PRAISE FOR **FIRST &**

MW00988807

"Amid brilliant and gorgeous nature writing, the collection aims to broaden traditional views of wilderness management—'to reimagine a land ethic that is inclusive, whole, and wild.' This anthology is a great addition to the literature of the American Southwest, natural history, and environmental conservation. It melds lush nature writing with thought-provoking calls for alternative environmental policies for the Gila and other national wilderness treasures."

—*FOREWORD REVIEWS*

"The Gila Wilderness is both a landmark in conservation history and a living, evolving place. *First & Wildest* is an elegant, impassioned, and timely tribute to its remarkable past and present."

—MICHELLE NIJHUIS, author of *Beloved Beasts*

"The Gila—and this great coterie of writers—tells us to know the earth, first know its wildness, a wildness that serves as the only path to our own true heart. Here, indeed, in the Gila Wilderness is the planet's essence."

—BOB SHACOCHIS, author of *Kingdoms in the Air* and *The Woman Who Lost Her Soul*

"Thorough, profound, multifaceted. Whether you call this place the Pueblo ancestral home or the Apache's Northern Stronghold or the Mexicans' stolen territory or the Anglos' wilderness, it's a range and a river that gives humans eternal gifts. Explore it here—then protect it forever."

—MARK SUNDEEN, author of *The Unsettlers*

"The Gila Wilderness occupies a seminal place in the history of conservation and the philosophy of land use. And now, as this awesome kingdom of rugged real estate approaches one hundred years of age as a preserve, here is an eloquent, lyrical, and exceedingly well-timed paean—a chorus of diverse voices, united in their love for this important and sometimes overlooked gem of the American Southwest."

—HAMPTON SIDES, *New York Times* bestselling
author of *Blood and Thunder*

"A century ago, the prehistoric beauty and rugged diversity of the Gila region of southwest New Mexico inspired a US Forest Service ranger to propose the creation of the Gila Wilderness, the first such designation in the United States. That ranger was the great naturalist Aldo Leopold, and as this engaging collection of writing shows, he was not alone among people stretching from ten thousand years ago till today to be deeply moved by the Gila's specialness or deeply alarmed by its fragility."

—ROBERT WILSON, editor, *The American Scholar*

FIRST
&
WILDEST

TORREY HOUSE PRESS

Salt Lake City • Torrey

FIRST
&
WILDEST

THE GILA WILDERNESS AT 100

EDITED BY
ELIZABETH
HIGHTOWER ALLEN

PHOTOGRAPHS BY
MICHAEL P. BERMAN

Inferno by Charles Bowden. Permission granted courtesy of the Charles Clyde Bowden Literary Trust. All rights reserved.

First Torrey House Press Edition, March 2022
Copyright © 2022 by Elizabeth Hightower Allen

All rights reserved. No part of this book may be reproduced or retransmitted in any form or by any means without the written consent of the publisher.

Published by Torrey House Press
Salt Lake City, Utah
www.torreyhouse.org

International Standard Book Number: 978-1-948814-55-3
E-book ISBN: 978-1-948814-56-0
Library of Congress Control Number: 2021941408

Cover photo by Michael P. Berman
Cover design by Kathleen Metcalf
Interior design by Rachel Buck-Cockayne
Distributed to the trade by Consortium Book Sales and Distribution

Torrey House Press offices in Salt Lake City sit on the homelands of Ute, Goshute, Shoshone, and Paiute nations. Offices in Torrey are on the homelands of Southern Paiute, Ute, and Navajo nations.

GILA NATIONAL WILDERNESS AREA

WILDERNESS AREA

HIGHWAY

PAVED ROAD

STATE LINE

GILA RIVER

■ TOWN / CITY

▲ MOUNTAIN / PEAK

NATIONAL FOREST

10 miles

Map created by

Vanessa Holz | Designer
vhdesign.graphics

Zach Scribner
GIS Analyst/Archaeologist
streamlinemaps.com

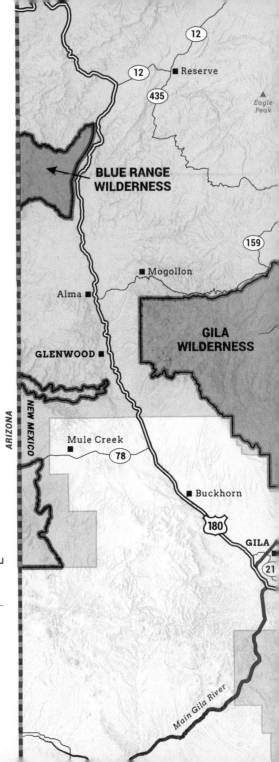

⑫

■ Reserve

⑫

④³⁵

▲ Eagle Peak

BLUE RANGE WILDERNESS

⑮⁹

■ Mogollon

Alma ■

GILA WILDERNESS

GLENWOOD ■

ARIZONA

NEW MEXICO

Mule Creek ■

⑦⁸

■ Buckhorn

180

GILA

㉑

Main Gila River

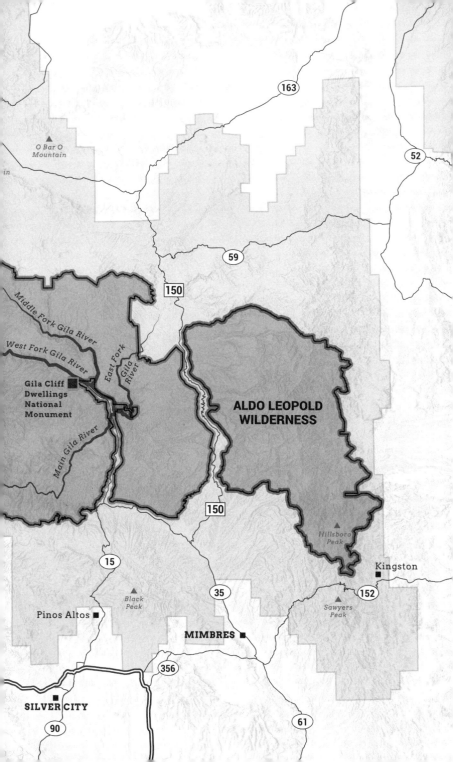

CONTENTS

HEAT
VOICES: CHARLES BOWDEN

FLOW
VOICES: M. H. DUTCH SALMON

conflict and trauma, unlocking the secrets of the Gila was more than just a trip to the forest."

FOREWORD

TOM UDALL

ONE HUNDRED YEARS AGO, ALDO LEOPOLD PROPOSED a novel and—as it turned out—brilliant, forward-looking idea. Leopold had worked for more than a decade in New Mexico for the fledgling US Forest Service, and had come to respect and love the untrammeled lands in the southwest part of the state we know as the Gila. Forty million years ago, super-volcanoes created one of the largest, most explosive, and longest-lasting volcanic activity in the world, spanning thirty-five million years. The formation of calderas, faulting, and erosion created the landscape that captivated Leopold as a young man: the high mesas, rolling hills, and deep canyons in the eastern portion; the sheer cliffs imposing upon the Gila River in the central area; and the high mountains of the Mogollon toward the west. He knew the piñon-juniper woodland and desert vegetation at the lower altitudes, the ponderosa pine as the elevation increased, and the spruce-fir and aspen forests above nine thousand feet.

Leopold understood earlier than most that maintaining natural balance in the system required protecting top predators like the wolf and mountain lion as well as the coati, javelina, and elk. "A thing is right when it tends to preserve the integrity, stability, and beauty of the biotic community. It is wrong when it tends otherwise," he wrote. He called this "thinking like a mountain." While the term *biodiversity* had yet to be coined, it was Leopold who first used *wilderness* to describe this indescribably magnificent place he wanted free of roads, logging, and mining.

Two years after Leopold proposed protecting this "ruggedly

beautiful country," the Forest Service set aside 558,014 acres of Gila Wilderness—the first wilderness in the nation.

First & Wildest: The Gila Wilderness at 100 tells the story of the Gila through the eyes of those like Leopold who love it: locals, descendants of its inhabitants, scientists, conservationists, recreationists.

I FIRST HIKED IN THE GILA in the mid-1970s, around when I was in law school at the University of New Mexico, and was last there a few years ago, when I was in the US Senate on a fact-finding mission related to proposals to divert the Gila River and to designate certain waters as wild and scenic. We hiked in and camped under the stars on the Gila River, and hiked to the San Francisco Peaks the next day. Hiking in the first day, we stopped at a rock ledge overlooking a picturesque bend in the Gila. Carved into the rock was a metate, a concave surface for grinding grain, possibly maize. I imagined the Mogollon inhabitants of hundreds of years ago sitting in our exact location, working away and taking in the same dramatic view of river we now so enjoyed.

Leopold and I were visitors to the Gila. But the headwaters of the Gila River have been home to Native peoples for millennia. Nomadic peoples used the caves of the Gila for thousands of years for temporary shelter. Around 1,450 years ago, people in what today is known as the Mimbres region began living a more sedentary lifestyle organized around pit-house villages. By 1150 CE, what archaeologists term the Mimbres Classic Period had ended, but the Chiricahua Apache people made their way to this place of abundance. The Apache or Nde people were attacked by or held an uneasy peace with the Spanish and then Mexicans until Mexico ceded the territory in 1848 after the Mexican-American War. The ancestral Nde lands were eventually taken by American soldiers, and the Apache forcibly relocated—a terrible and unjust action repeated over and over throughout our history.

Recognition of the immense archaeological and cultural value of the Gila Cliff Dwellings followed. The area that contained these five caves became one of the first national monuments designated under the Antiquities Act of 1906. These ancient dwellings and the Gila River represent the heart of the Gila Wilderness.

The Gila was the first Wilderness, but not the last. There are now over eight hundred Wilderness areas across the nation. Leopold would be proud that his idea of preserving "wilderness" took hold. And I'm proud that my father, Stewart Udall, when he was secretary of the Department of the Interior, helped lead passage of the Wilderness Act of 1964. Today, more than 110 million acres of our wildest places that are "without permanent improvements or human habitation" are "protected and managed so as to preserve [their] natural conditions."

But we have so much more work to do—designating more wild places for permanent protection, moving with all urgency and purpose to tackle climate change, and continuing to safeguard the astounding biodiversity of the Gila.

WE ARE ON A PRECIPICE. Scientists tell us we must save 30 percent of our planet's lands and waters by 2030, and 50 percent by 2050, to save nature as we know it. We are in the middle of a human-caused mass extinction of plant and animal species. The world has lost two-thirds of global animal, bird, and fish populations over the past fifty years. We must protect more wild lands and waters to stop this crisis—not only to save the planet's flora and fauna, but to save ourselves. Nature provides our life support system—our food, shelter, medicine, and economic development. As my father put it decades ago: "Plans to protect air and water, wilderness and wildlife are, in fact, plans to protect [humankind]."

Climate change is here and now and, in the arid Southwest,

New Mexico is right in the bull's-eye—with temperatures rising, drought on our doorstep, snowpack and spring runoff anemic, and wildfires threatening. The Whitewater-Baldy Fire shot through the Gila in the summer of 2012 and, at almost three hundred thousand acres, remains the largest fire in our state's history. We have the technology and science to reverse course. We have the technology to get to zero carbon emissions. We must muster the political will to replace fossil fuels with renewable sources and ratchet up our energy conservation and efficiency.

As we take on the interrelated nature and climate crises, environmental justice must be our north star. We must look through the diversity, equity, and inclusion lens with each and every environmental policy we adopt and decision we make. As we move forward, firmly committed to racial justice, we must grapple with our past—like the injustice done to the Apache people whose Gila home was taken from them.

Our work in the Gila is not done. In 2014, tragedy struck when three Silver City teens, monitoring forest health in the Gila, lost their young lives when the plane they were in crashed. I met a number of times with the parents of sixteen-year-old Ella Myers, sixteen-year-old Michael Mahl, and fourteen-year-old Ella Kirk. The teens' parents carry on their children's commitment to the Gila. These exceptional young people inspire me, and I hope inspire others, to safeguard the wild lands that Aldo Leopold set out to protect from human destruction a century ago. We had a recent victory—stopping the major diversion on the Gila River and keeping it free-flowing in New Mexico. A next step is protecting the Gila and San Francisco rivers and their tributaries by giving them the highest level of protection Congress can bestow: protecting them as wild and scenic under the Wild and Scenic Rivers Act. Senator Martin Heinrich and I introduced the M. H. Dutch Salmon Greater Gila Wild and Scenic River Act in 2020. Named for longtime Gila conservation advocate Dutch Salmon, who passed away in 2019, the legislation would designate almost 450 miles of Gila waters as wild and scenic. Senators Heinrich and Ben Ray Luján are carrying that legislation forward.

The Gila Wilderness is the most biologically diverse area in New Mexico—home to fourteen native fish, including four not found anywhere else in the world; to the bobcat, cougar, mule deer, black bear, gray fox; and to some of the greatest bird diversity in the Southwest. For decades, the Gila has drawn locals and is one of New Mexico's most popular outdoor destinations—attracting birders, hikers, rafters, kayakers, fishers, and hunters. We should all commit to what Aldo Leopold helped start and to what Ella, Michael, and Ella continued—protecting the uniquely New Mexican Gila Wilderness.

INTRODUCTION

ELIZABETH HIGHTOWER ALLEN

W E DROVE THE FORTY-ONE MILES FROM SILVER City to Gila Hot Springs in fading October light, expecting the last leg of the trip from Santa Fe to take about an hour. It took more than two. I'd never been to the Gila before, and I knew the place was rugged—but not like this. Instead of traveling along valley floors and over low passes, like a mountain road with any sense, Highway 15 crept along the tops of the ridgelines themselves. Steep, rocky inclines slid away on either side of the road, with only cloud shadows to interrupt the wide expanse of distant ranges and windswept burn scars.

Aldo Leopold was likewise blown away when he arrived in the Gila National Forest in 1909 as a young ranger for the US Forest Service. Yet even back then, he watched the encroachment of human impacts on the land: erosion from overgrazing and fire suppression, new roads for recreational and logging use. What if, he proposed to his Forest Service colleagues in 1922, we set aside some of that land, never to be developed with roads or recreational facilities or anything at all. What if, he argued, we left a few places to themselves? In his essay "Wilderness and its Place in Forest Recreational Policy," published in 1921 in the *Journal of Forestry*, Leopold explained how he defined the term. "By 'wilderness,'" he wrote, "I mean a continuous stretch of country preserved in its natural state, open to lawful hunting and fishing, big enough to absorb a two weeks' pack trip, and kept devoid of roads, artificial trails, cottages, or other works of man."

The title of that essay didn't have a lot going for it, but the idea was radical. To draw a line around what is sacred and inviolate and has been to many cultures for thousands of years, and say, *This is not for us.* And to hold that line for a century and counting.

The area Leopold had in mind was 870 square miles surrounding the headwaters of the Gila River, from spruce-fir forests above nine thousand feet down to piñon-juniper scrub in the lower elevations and willow and cottonwood in the riparian areas. In 1924, the Forest Service officially created the Gila Wilderness—America's first, the world's first. A century later, that first patch of Wilderness has grown to include 111 million acres across every American ecosystem.

To commemorate not just the centennial of the Gila Wilderness, but of wilderness with a capital *W*, Torrey House Press has joined with WildEarth Guardians to create this book. *First & Wildest* seeks not only to celebrate the Gila, but to explore the looming threats of extinction and climate change altering this landscape. It is a celebration of everything the Gila Wilderness has inspired—and a call to action to find inspiration once again in this birthplace of the wilderness ideal.

I'M NOT THE ONLY PERSON who took a while to get to the Gila. It is one of our most remote, inaccessible wilderness areas, one that few Americans have ever penetrated very far.

So let's start with the basics. At 558,065 acres, the Gila isn't the largest federally designated wilderness. Alaska's Wrangell-St. Elias Wilderness claims that title, with 9,078,675 million acres. The Gila isn't as famous as the Boundary Waters in Minnesota, or the Maroon Bells in Colorado. But it is one of the most rugged stretches in the Lower 48. To the east is the Aldo Leopold Wilderness, 202,016 acres of the igneous Black Range. To the west, crossing into Arizona, is the 29,304-acre Blue Range Wilderness, which bleeds into Arizona's 199,505-acre Blue Range Primitive Area. And it doesn't stop with federal designation. Even on its fringes, this is rough, rough country. The Greater Gila Bioregion—what we generally mean when we say "the Gila"—is twice the size of New Jersey, 10 million acres extending east to New Mexico's Black Range, north to El Malpais National Monument, west to the White Mountains of Arizona, and south to the Sonoran and Chihuahuan Deserts. It's both larger and more biodiverse than Yellowstone National Park yet includes 1.5 million roadless acres that are still unprotected.

The most famous resident of that landscape, of course, is the Mexican gray wolf, the lobo, which was reintroduced in 1998 after being wiped out by the 1970s. Today, 186 wolves make the Greater Gila their home. They are joined by (newly nervous) elk, beaver, bobcat, gray fox, ringtail cat, mule deer, coyote, black bear, javelina, and those curious monkey-raccoon creatures called coati—as well as the eponymous Gila woodpecker, Gila chub, Gila trout, and Gila monster.

Today, however, the twin crises of climate change and species loss are bearing down upon the Greater Gila in the form of megadrought, megafire, and an ever-increasing list of threatened and endangered species. Mining exploration and commercial livestock grazing continue to broaden their reach. Everywhere there are dry grasses and dry creekbeds, and dry lightning to set it all aflame.

THE WORLD HAS OBVIOUSLY CHANGED a lot since Leopold first rode up into the Gila River headwaters on horseback. Cultural critics have questioned the idea of wilderness as yet another example of Western colonialism and patriarchy. How very brash, how American, to roll up on a landscape that has been traveled by Indigenous peoples for more than twenty thousand years and proclaim that its use has been redefined. The United

States is not the first culture to move through this space. Ancestors of modern Native people—including but not limited to the Hopi, Zuni, and Acoma Pueblos—thrived in the Gila, part of the ancient Mimbres and Mogollon cultures. The Apache people still do. Geronimo was born in these forests. Many generations of ranchers, both Hispanic and Anglo, have worked this land.

Yet Leopold himself did not see the definition of wilderness as fixed. As he would write decades later in *A Sand County Almanac*, "I have purposely presented the land ethic as a product of social evolution because nothing so important as an ethic is ever written....It evolves in the minds of a thinking community."

We have gathered members of that community in the pages that follow. They include politicians, poets, biologists, biographers, horsepackers and fire lookouts, archaeologists and administrators. They are Anglo, Apache, Mexican American, and all of the above. And the Gila means different things to each of them.

To Pam Houston, the Gila calls to mind the line between the hunter and the hunted, the question of whether there is room in modern America for the wolf. To Philip Connors, it's home in a fire lookout tower for much of the year, watching for the flames that shape the land. To Leeanna T. Torres, it's a place without easy definition, where a biologist must kill one kind of trout to save another. And to Priscilla Solis Ybarra, it is a reminder, through the Mexican American heritage of the Leopold family, that conservation is not as white as it seems. To Beto O'Rourke, it's a gift from his father to pass down to his own children. And to Joe Saenz, the Gila was, and remains today, the Northern Stronghold of the Chiricahua Apache Tribe.

To all of them, the Greater Gila represents one of our last opportunities to reimagine a land ethic that is inclusive, whole, and wild. The problems are big but the possibilities hopeful. What should the Gila look like in another hundred years? Can expanded protection for this Yellowstone of the Southwest assure more resilience for its wild animals and tangled beauty?

The Gila isn't an easy place to get to know. That's a big part of its allure, and to be frank, its value. But over time, it reveals itself as irreplaceable. Personally, I have only scratched its surface, but in these pages, I feel that I've experienced some of its most closely held secrets. I hope you will feel the same.

EVE WEST BESSIER

ODE TO THE GILA

Wilderness

a remote place without roads

a vigorous place thriving long before roads

a venerable place where human access
is limited or non-existent

a verdant place where native species grow
or wander on meandering animal trails

a wild place where the wind agitates and whines
in the long-needled canopy of ponderosa pines
while sturdy piñon and emory oak remain still
and slender lip ferns, aster and penstemon gently nod
two hundred feet below on the composted forest floor

Here, flicker and thresher melodies flute in spring
accented by the hammering of pileated woodpeckers
and the high cries of nesting golden eagles
recently returned from their southern wintering

The nearly extinct Mexican gray wolf now howls
to a waning moon, prowling for pronghorn,

elk and white-tailed deer in the ebbing twilight
as bighorn sheep, bobcat, javelina and beaver
keep their ancient rites and seasonal rituals

Rare and at-risk species are returning here,
Mexican spotted owls, Gila hot springs snails,
Chiricahua leopard frogs, recently even jaguars

In this wilderness, protected now for a century
three forks of the Gila River sing of water over stone
while persistent winds slip over ridges
forecasting change and the shifting tides
of strong jet streams over the Great Divide

Wilderness

a distant place far from the reach of humans, yet
a fragile place where humans fought
to save a river from being dammed,
to save the silent cobalt sky from being blasted
by the roar of military fighter jets training overhead

Wilderness

a secretive place, elusive in natural history
where sheer vastness creates its own sanctuary
and the Mogollon Mountains draw a long crescent
across an almost impassable expanse

From the vantage point of the Aldo Leopold lookout
the Gila towers over yucca-speckled rangeland
with formidable, craggy peaks that do not extend
a friendly invitation, but hide their treasures behind
unclimbable heights and jagged, barren buttresses

We who live in close proximity can savor
the Gila's beauty at its outer boundaries
on trails in the national forest that provide
the ardent day hiker views of emerald valleys

In spring and summer we may encounter
Continental Divide Trail through-hikers
walking from Mexico to Canada, passing
near to the heart of the Gila in hiking boots
with only their heavy backpacks and GPS maps

The Gila is our nation's first wilderness
now part of the larger 3.3 million acre
Gila National Forest, it is guarded to remain pristine,
experienced directly only by avid naturalists, fly-fishers
and photographers willing to pack in on horseback

True, tourists can reach the Gila Cliff Dwellings
and the hot springs by driving a winding road
and cyclists race along the precarious edge
of an ancient caldera once every year

but mostly, the Gila is a place
where nature remembers
her purest forms
her most private riches

her own quiet wildness

BEDROCK

100

"Everything depends on our ability to sustainably inhabit this earth, and true sustainability will require us all to change our way of thinking on how we take from the earth and how we give back."

—Deb Haaland
US Secretary of the Interior
"More than Politics—It's Personal,"
Medium, September 26, 2017

ALDO LEOPOLD

THE WILDERNESS AND ITS PLACE
IN FOREST RECREATIONAL POLICY

Leopold published this article in the Journal of Forestry *in 1921 and subsequently included it in his proposal to the US Forest Service to create a designated wilderness area in the Gila National Forest. Leopold's conception of wilderness would continue to evolve, but as editors David E. Brown and Neil B. Carmony write in the 1990 collection* Aldo Leopold's Southwest, *it "led directly to the establishment of America's first wilderness area in 1924, and eventually to one of the most profound pieces of conservation legislation of the 20th century—the Wilderness Act of 1964."*

WHEN THE NATIONAL FORESTS WERE CREATED THE first argument of those opposing a national forest policy was that the forests would remain a wilderness. Gifford Pinchot [the first chief of the Forest Service] replied that on the contrary they would be opened up and developed as producing forests, and that such development would, in the long run, itself constitute the best assurance that they would neither remain a wilderness by "bottling up" their resources nor become one through devastation. At this time Pinchot enunciated the doctrine of "highest use," and its criterion, "the greatest good to the greatest number," which is and must remain the guiding principle by which democracies handle their natural resources.

Pinchot's promise of development has been made good. The process must, of course, continue indefinitely. But it has already gone far enough to raise the question of whether the policy of development (construed in the narrower sense of industrial development) should continue to govern in absolutely every instance, or whether the principle of highest use does not itself demand that representative portions of some forests be preserved as wilderness.

That some such question actually exists, both in the minds of some foresters and of part of the public, seems to me to be plainly implied in the recent trend of recreational use policies and in the tone of sporting and outdoor magazines. Recreational plans are leaning toward the segregation of certain areas from certain developments, so that having been led into the wilderness, the people may have some wilderness left to enjoy. Sporting magazines are groping toward some logical reconciliation between getting back to nature and preserving a little nature to get back to. Lamentations over this or that favorite vacation ground being "spoiled by tourists" are becoming more and more frequent. Very evidently we have here the old conflict between preservation and use, long since an issue with respect to timber, water power, and other purely economic resources, but just now coming to be an issue with respect to recreation. It is the fundamental function of foresters to reconcile these conflicts, and to give constructive direction to these issues as they arise. The purpose of this paper is to give definite form to the issue of wilderness conservation, and to suggest certain policies for meeting it, especially as applied to the Southwest.

It is quite possible that the serious discussion of this question will seem a far cry in some unsettled regions, and rank heresy to some minds. Likewise did timber conservation seem a far cry in some regions, and rank heresy to some minds of a generation ago. "The truth is that which prevails in the long run."

Some definitions are probably necessary at the outset. By "wilderness" I mean a continuous stretch of country preserved in its natural state, open to lawful hunting and fishing, big enough to absorb a two weeks' pack trip, and kept devoid of roads, artificial trails, cottages, or other works of man. Several assumptions can be made at once without argument. First, such wilderness areas should occupy only a small fraction of the total National Forest area—probably not to exceed one in each State. Second, only areas naturally difficult of ordinary industrial development should be chosen. Third, each area should be representative of some type of country of distinctive recreational value, or afford some distinctive type of outdoor life, opportunity for which might disappear on other forest lands open to industrial development.

The argument for such wilderness areas is premised wholly on highest recreational use. The recreational desires and needs of the public, whom the forests must serve, vary greatly with the individual. Heretofore we have been inclined to assume that our recreational development policy must be based on the desires and needs of the majority only. The only new thing about the premise in this case is the proposition that in as much as we have plenty of room and plenty of time, it is our duty to vary our recreational development policy, in some places, to meet the needs and desires of the minority also. The majority undoubtedly want all the automobile roads, summer hotels, graded trails, and other modern conveniences that we can give them. It is already decided, and wisely, that they shall have these things as rapidly as brains and money can provide them. But a very substantial minority, I think, want just the opposite. It should be decided, as soon as the existence of the demand can be definitely determined, to provide what this minority wants. In fact, if we can foresee the demand, and make provision for it in advance, it will save much cash and hard feelings. It will be much easier to keep wilderness areas than to create them. In fact, the latter alternative may be dismissed as impossible. Right here is the whole reason for forehandedness in the proposed wilderness area policy.

It is obvious to everyone who knows the National Forests that even with intensive future development, there will be a decreasing but inexhaustible number of small patches of rough country which will remain practically in wilderness condition. It is also generally recognized that these small patches have a high and increasing recreational value. But will they obviate the need for a policy such as here proposed? I think not. These patches are too small, and must grow smaller. They will always be big enough for camping, but they will tend to grow too small for a real wilderness trip. The public demands for camp sites and wilderness trips, respectively, are both legitimate and both strong, but nevertheless distinct. The man who wants a wilderness trip wants not only scenery, hunting, fishing, isolation, etc.—all of which can often be found within a mile of a paved auto highway—but also the horses, packing, riding, daily movement and variety found only in a trip through a big stretch of wild country. It would be pretty lame to forcibly import these features into a country from which the real need for them had disappeared.

It may also be asked whether the National Parks from which, let us hope, industrial development will continue to be excluded, do not fill the public demand here discussed. They do, in part. But hunting is not and should not be allowed within the Parks. Moreover, the Parks are being networked with roads and trails as rapidly as possible. This is right and proper. The Parks merely prove again that the recreational needs and desires of the public vary through a wide range of individual tastes, all of which should be met in due proportion to the number of individuals in each class. There is only one question involved—highest use. And we are beginning to see that highest use is a very varied use, requiring a very varied administration, in the recreational as well as in the industrial field.

An actual example is probably the best way to describe the workings of the proposed wilderness area policy.

The Southwest (meaning New Mexico and Arizona) is a distinct region. The original southwestern wilderness was the scene of several important chapters in our national history. The remainder of it is about as interesting, from about as large a number of angles, as any place on the continent. It has a high and varied recreational value. Under the policy advocated in this paper, a good big sample of it should be preserved. This could easily be done by selecting such an area as the headwaters of the Gila River on the Gila National Forest. This is an area of nearly half a million acres, topographically isolated by mountain ranges and box canyons. It has not yet been penetrated by railroads and to only a very limited extent by roads. On account of the natural obstacles to transportation and the absence of any considerable areas of agricultural land, no net economic loss would result from the policy of withholding further industrial development, except that the timber would remain inaccessible and available only for limited local consumption. The entire area is grazed by cattle, but the cattle ranches would be an asset from the recreational standpoint because of the interest which attaches to cattle grazing operations under frontier conditions. The apparent disadvantage thus imposed on the cattlemen might be nearly offset by the obvious advantage of freedom from new settlers, and from the hordes of motorists who will invade this region the minute it is opened up. The entire region is the natural habitat of deer, elk, turkey, grouse, and trout. If preserved in its semi-virgin state, it could absorb a hundred pack trains each year without overcrowding. It is the last typical wilderness in the southwestern mountains. Highest use demands its preservation.

The conservation of recreational resources here advocated has its historic counterpart in the conservation of timber resources lately become a national issue and expressed in the forestry program. Timber conservation began fifteen years ago with the same vague preconditions of impending shortage now discernible in the recreational press. Timber conservation encountered the same general rebuttal of "inexhaustible supplies" which recreational conservation will shortly encounter. After a period of milling and mulling, timber conservation established the principle that timber supplies are capable of qualitative as well as quantitative exhaustion, and that the existence of "inexhaustible" areas of trees did not necessarily insure the supply of bridge timber, naval stores, or pulp. So also will recreational resources be found in more danger of qualitative than quantitative exhaustion. We now recognize that the sprout forests of New England are no answer to the farmer's need for structural lumber, and we admit that the farmer's special needs must be taken care of in proportion to his numbers and importance. So also must we recognize that any number of small patches of uninhabited wood or mountains are no answer to the real sportsman's need for wilderness, and the day will come when we must admit that his special needs likewise must be taken care of in proportion to his numbers and importance. And as in forestry, it will be much easier and cheaper to preserve, by forethought, what he needs, than to create it after it is gone.

JOE SAENZ
AS TOLD TO ALASTAIR LEE BITSÓÍ

NDE BENAH

NDE BENAH. THIS IS APACHE LAND. MANY KNOW IT AS the Gila Wilderness, Gila National Forest, Aldo Leopold Wilderness, and Blue Range Wilderness. As Nde people, it is our Northern Stronghold. Our history, culture, and language run deep into this landscape of mountains, canyons, and grasslands. These are the traditional lands and country to the Warm Springs Band of Chiricahua Apaches, of which I'm a descendant.

I have been privileged to live in my traditional lands. It took me a while to really understand the importance of Nde lands. Traveling around and living in different places for a while, I relearned the value of how to live in and appreciate this country. To be part of a group of people that treated this land as it should be, as we were instructed by the Creator, protecting all its functions and all its parts—the animals, the water, the soil, the trees.

When I say "country," I am referring to the Northern Stronghold, ancestral Nde lands. Most of the Gila National Forest is Nde lands, as well as areas now known as Apache, Cibola, and Coronado National Forests in southern New Mexico. The four bands that make up the Chiricahua Apache extended all the way from I-40 three hundred miles south into Mexico, all the way from the Sacramento and Guadalupe Mountains west to Tucson. The Warm Springs Band, my band, mostly inhabited the Black Range and the eastern side of the Gila Wilderness, all the way to the Rio Grande.

Now I see all these place names associated with the Gila

Wilderness and within the Gila National Forest, and they have nothing to do with Apache. Or, if they do, these names are very derogatory or disrespectful. I've asked our elders what they remember. What is their story of this country?

My great-grandmother used to talk about this quite a bit, how the northern mountains are the Northern Stronghold—the entire Gila Wilderness and Gila National Forest—and how the Southern Stronghold is down in the Sierra Madres. One elder, a descendant of Mangas Coloradas, confirmed this area being our Northern Stronghold. There is a word for this area, *Huułi*, meaning "where things originate, or come from," and this is the cultural knowledge from my elders and ancestors.

Our stories tell us that we were created here. We believe there were many points of emergence throughout the world. And there was one right here. Archaeologists and anthropologists give credit to the Puebloan peoples, who passed through the area and left their ancestral structures, like cliff dwellings, pit houses, and petroglyphs. All of their footprints were left behind. As they passed through, we contend that they came from a different direction, the south; we do not ascribe to the land bridge theory. I grew up hearing a different story. My grandparents told me stories of how Indigenous peoples moved in this area, where they came from, who was here, and who was not. And so those truths were ingrained in me. When I attended college, of course I heard differently. And I'm going, "Wait a minute. I heard it differently."

So yes, there are Ancestral Puebloan sites here, and we know they moved from the region. But we were here, and we can attest to that. The only people that were able to run us off were the US government and the US military. They did that by trickery, by genocide, and by conventional war. But this is Apache land, and always has been.

We lived off this land. We did not have to grow crops. We did not have rock buildings. There was a way to move through this country to flourish. We had a variety of terrain that accommodated us in winter and summer, plenty of carrying capacity for all of us. Aside from the physical beauty, the mountains, we had the minerals, the timber, the forest, the lowlands with desert and cactus—all of that accommodated us, nourished us, and gave us the spiritual connection.

As Nde, we wove ourselves through these environments because we understood that damaging any system would damage other parts of the ecosystem, and would eventually cause damage to us, so it was important that our movement accommodated that. The philosophies, the medicine, all of that, manifested itself in those lives. Just amazing.

THERE IS A REASON MOST of this country is national forest. The dominant society, also known as Americans, saw these lands from a monetary perspective. But it is impossible to care for this land without the knowledge of our Nde connections and acknowledgment of the Nde as the guardians of this cultural landscape. When comparing Indigenous views and Western perspectives, there is a distorted perception. On the one hand, we are the voice to speak against exploitation of this land for its timber, water, grass, or any of its other elements. Settlers, however, want to use Nde lands for monetary gain.

Instead of calling it the Gila Wilderness, I very much prefer it as the Apache Preserve. That would be a starting point to reclaiming *Nde benah*, with Apache values, ideology, and culture. Understanding how to manage these lands from our view would help the state and federal governments learn that these lands are sacred. Instead of knowing the latitude and longitude of a specific sacred site, it is the whole country. Our values of what is sacred—both tangible and intangible—run counter to American government and its political system.

There's really no intrinsic monetary value that goes with

our culture. We moved around too much, a value that cannot be capitalized upon. What are we going to do, make bows and arrows on a street corner? When outsiders visit the area, it is marketed as Puebloan culture, and people line up in carloads to see the remnants of what outsiders think is a dead culture, and so there is no responsibility and accountability to those Indigenous narratives. And so that culture is perpetuated; hence, the need for responsibility and accountability. Apache people lived differently and are still present in the area.

We're here to say there is a different way to experience the Northern Stronghold. Imagine this country without those petroglyphs. Imagine this country without those cliff dwellings. Imagine this country without those pit houses. That's what we saw. And now this landscape is changing, especially under the management of the Forest Service. We are extremely lucky to have the Gila Wilderness and Gila National Forest. We're able to hang on. But the wilderness has been in decline due to mismanagement since the land was taken over in the late 1800s.

One of the threats is fire. Fire is a big business. Money. Everything is done around fire now. They need to stop fighting fires in the wilderness and just monitor them.

That's what we deal with here in the wilderness. Priorities change. I see those changes happening. The whole idea with the first rangers was multiple use—let's log it, hunt it, let's do all this. The miners, hunters, and trappers killed everything here— the elk, the deer, the grizzly, the wolf. They destroyed the ecosystems, and now they want to play God and bring back these sacred beings. That has always been an interesting way to think: *Let's use it until it's gone. Then let's try to bring it back.*

Well, what if you started with life to begin with?

RIGHT NOW, THERE IS A growing trend among our peoples to reclaim our traditional territory in the Gila region. We are seeing more and more Nde and ancestral Nde move back to the area from places like Oklahoma and California, having been forcibly removed through federal policies of relocation. With a growing presence of Nde peoples, we are also experiencing some backlash in our own territory, in part because we are shifting the narrative with Indigenous history, culture, and language.

While we continue to amplify Apache connections to the Gila, we are also on the frontlines organizing around issues that negatively impact this pristine and sacred country. The last stand we took was stopping the damming of the Gila River and the flyovers of the US Air Force, which uses the Gila landscape as training grounds for the military. I want to encourage our allies and friends to continue opposing these flyovers, because this territory is asking us to protect it in an effort to achieve balance. I told people in the community, we tried a long time ago to step up and protect this country. We're still here, we're still fighting. Now it's your turn. You need to step in and help if you really value this country. As Nde, we want a seat at the table, and hope that the modern land managers—the Bureau of Land Management and US Forest Service—allow us this opportunity to get involved with the planning and decision-making.

Some believe that this country holds a great power for us. It's been broken; it's been severed. What we are trying to do is remake that connection.

As Indigenous people, we know what this land was like before it was colonized by settlers. There were no roads or electric lines. It was a complete wilderness. And as we lived in this space, the perception of what is now wilderness had, and continues to have, a different meaning. Today, wilderness is seen as a place where humans do not belong. If you call it the Gila Wilderness, it should be managed in such a way—as an interactive wilderness that will help teach people. Not as a park for rich travelers and the creation of man-made structures because they are losing sight of what is really there.

HOW MY ANCESTORS LIVED WAS through expressing their connections to the world and the Creator. They flourished through our songs and dances, and through honoring the plants, the animals, everything that gave them sustenance. That is true freedom. One of the reasons we were so threatening to American society is that we know the difference between the reality of freedom and the illusion of freedom. As Native people, we had true freedom. That lifestyle is embodied into who we are. Today everyone is into titles—wanting to be an architect, doctor, or some other profession. This is good, but as Apache we think of how we can be the best Apache person we can be. And that requires following the standards and protocols set by our ancestors: how they lived and survived, their knowledge of medicines, food, and everything that makes us Apache.

I run a horse-riding business throughout the Gila, and though I consider the horse to be one of the most destructive animals to the landscape, I make sure to have as little impact as possible. On my trips, we move daily. We do not stay in one spot for too long. If I come across an area where there is very little water, I work with my horses so they can tolerate the dryness. I'll leave the water for the animals—the birds, elk, and deer. But even that pales compared to what our ancestors did, who set the highest standards of living. We have to work toward those standards because they really are strong.

The value of the wilderness is not just visual. To us, it wasn't just, *Oh, beautiful mountains. Nice river.* It was nourishment, life. In modern America, it's perceived as, *Why are you saving that land? Well, it's pretty and I can drive through it. Maybe we could camp there for a night.* But you ask an Apache, and they say, *We used to eat that over there. We slept in this country. We traveled here because we knew there was water.* It's a whole different connection that goes much deeper than just aesthetics, than what America seems to be clamoring for.

As we have told people, even though we may have lost

physical possession of this country, we still retain 100 percent of the spiritual ownership of this land. No matter how many monuments you build, and how many beautiful homes, you are never going to have the beauty of the land itself. It does not need improvement. As Creator gave it to us, it is in its perfect form. We need to take care of it. This is Apache Land. *Nde Benah.*

JAKOB W. SEDIG

LESSONS IN RESILIENCE

FIRST WITNESSED THE GILA WILDERNESS THROUGH THE cracked windshield of my stick-shift 2001 GMC Sonoma pickup truck. It was January 2011, and I was a graduate student in search of a dissertation research project.

I'd spent the first part of my archaeological career in the northern reaches of the US Southwest, at Chacoan sites like Chimney Rock. But I wanted to work further south. So I devoted part of my winter break to exploring the Mimbres region, which stretches north-south from Reserve, New Mexico, to Chihuahua, Mexico, and east-west from the Rio Grande to about Safford, Arizona.

Like most people, the main thing I knew about the Mimbres culture was that, around one thousand years ago, they made black (and red) on white bowls that featured uncanny images of people, animals, and other figures. And I knew that, though looters had devastated the vast majority of Mimbres sites in search of these bowls, there was still much to learn about this ancient culture.

It takes about eleven hours to get from Boulder, Colorado (where I was a graduate student), to the Mimbres heartland, with about nine hours on I-25 South. After Truth or Consequences, you can continue down I-25 a bit longer and then take NM-26 West, stopping at Sparky's in Hatch for a green chile cheeseburger. Or you can cut west just past T or C on NM-152, which crosses into the Gila National Forest and through the Black Range. Fortunately, I chose this option.

Although it was my first drive through the Gila, I remember having a sense of déjà vu, at least partially attributable to the numerous curves and switchbacks that can seem indistinguishable from one another, especially after nine hours on the road. Although I'd spent half a decade bumming around the forests, mountains, and deserts of the northern Southwest, the Gila seemed different. An intangible weight surrounded me. The forest felt wild, primordial. This first immersion was different from how I would later experience the forest. Most of my drives over the Black Range have since been during the spring and summer—prime archaeology seasons—but this traverse was in winter. My Sonoma almost got hung up in a snowbank when I stopped to take in the view from Emory Pass.

BY FAR THE BEST-KNOWN ARCHAEOLOGICAL site in southwest New Mexico is the Gila Cliff Dwellings, built at the end of the thirteenth century. But they were a one-off—an extended family (or two) lived there for only a generation (or two) before moving on.

I was drawn instead to a site called Woodrow Ruin, about twenty miles southwest of the Cliff Dwellings, on a bench above the floodplain where the Gila River emerges from the Upper Box. Woodrow is one of the largest sites in the Mimbres core, which consists of the upper Gila and Mimbres River Valleys. Evidence at Woodrow pointed to a long, continuous occupation, through the Mimbres Late Pithouse (CE 550-1000) and Classic (CE 1000-1130) periods. And, just like modern inhabitants of southwest New Mexico, the people who lived at Woodrow were vulnerable to the impacts of a temperamental environment.

I'd spend the next three summers doing fieldwork at Woodrow. During the 2012 Whitewater-Baldy Fire, I watched smoke pillars rise skyward while I sifted excavated fill looking for ceramic sherds, stone tools, and the remnants of plants and animals that Woodrow's inhabitants consumed. These artifacts, along with other data collected from the site, shed new light onto the resilience of the ancient Mimbres culture.

Drought and fire are part of life in arid environments; the inhabitants of southwest New Mexico have been dealing with them since the ancestors of modern-day Native people first arrived over 20,000 years ago. However, one drought in particular, around 1,100 years ago, was the worst in millennia.

ARCHAEOLOGISTS EMPLOY A VARIETY OF METHODS—soil coring, ice coring, and exciting new techniques like sequencing DNA— to reconstruct ancient environments. Tree-ring data can also be used to glimpse what the conditions were like centuries or millennia ago. Tree rings grow thick during moist years. When precipitation is low, rings are narrow. Due to its aridity, the US Southwest is blessed with an unmatched tree-ring record. Using this record (and some other techniques), archaeologists and environmental scientists have determined that around 900 CE, the rains diminished significantly in central and southern New Mexico. While there were years of reprieve, the subsequent one hundred years were abnormally dry.

When the drought first struck, people who called southwest New Mexico home resided in below-ground structures called pit houses. Most communities were small, consisting of a handful of extended families, united through ritual activities held in large, subterranean communal structures called great kivas. People grew maize, but they harvested plenty of wild resources, too. By the end of the drought, around 1000 CE, Mimbres society had entirely transformed. People had started building above-ground, pueblo-style room blocks. Wide-open plazas that could accommodate large gatherings replaced great kivas, which were closed and had limited capacity. Many great kivas were abandoned or burned in ritual closing ceremonies. Maize became a more central part of the diet. Hundreds of people lived at the largest villages. It was during this time that Mimbres people started producing the iconic ceramic bowls that featured vivid images of plants, animals, or intricate geometric designs.

Archaeologists have been aware of the differences between the Late Pithouse and Classic periods for almost as long as archaeological research has been conducted in southwest New Mexico. Yet the transition between the two periods has been poorly understood. Because looters hadn't entirely devastated Woodrow, there was clear evidence of the so-called pit house to pueblo transition. My work at Woodrow examined this "transitional" phase. Work at the site demonstrated a large, continuous occupation from the Late Pithouse through Classic periods and defined how domestic architecture evolved from pit houses to pueblos. Data from Woodrow, combined with other data from the Mimbres region, have helped create a better understanding of this transformative period.

I don't think it coincidental that Mimbres society underwent a dramatic transformation in the midst of a century-long drought. However, I'm not an environmental determinist—the drought wasn't the sole causal factor for the plethora of transformations between the Late Pithouse and Classic periods. There is strong evidence that dramatically changing religious practices drove many of those changes—the switch from great kivas to plazas, the flowering of Mesoamerican ideology, and new meaning embedded in domestic architecture. New religious beliefs and practices would have served as a palliative during a severe, extended drought, but these transformations were also tied to waning connections with the Hohokam people (in modern-day Arizona), and waxing interaction with burgeoning Chaco Canyon and Mesoamerican cultures.

Archaeologists have uncovered myriad examples of ancient cultures that had deleterious responses to drought. Often, extreme drought is correlated with famine, violence, and abandonment. This wasn't the case for the tenth-century inhabitants of the Mimbres, who found ways to flourish during this pro-longed hardship. Instead of fighting each other over dwindling resources or fleeing their homeland, they altered their socio-religious systems and were able to persist. People were flexible; over the course of one hundred years, their society totally transformed itself. This transformation, largely associated with ritual beliefs and practices, almost certainly helped people cope with environmental stress.

The inhabitants of the Mimbres region responded quite differently to a less severe drought at the end of the Classic period, in the mid-1100s CE. By this point, the population had grown significantly, and there is some evidence of emerging social hierarchy, particularly associated with control of prime agricultural lands. People practiced extensive maize farming, which degraded cultivated areas, and wild resources were increasingly depleted. Forests in the northern reaches of the Mimbres region, today's Gila National Forest, were almost certainly denuded. In essence, Mimbres society had become more rigid than it was two hundred years prior. By 1150 CE, the Mimbres region was largely depopulated, with people moving to the east and south.

MODERN AMERICAN SOCIETY MUST BE flexible if we are to avoid the fighting, famine, and fleeing that so often seem to accompany environmental downturns in the archaeological record. We must dramatically alter how our homes are constructed and consume energy; we need to adopt practices that appreciate our natural surroundings; we must change the way we produce and distribute food; and we must continue to protect places like the Gila.

Although I am a public-lands advocate, my research on the ancestors of modern-day Native Americans has made me acutely aware of the more problematic aspects of a place I love. The Gila Wilderness has been protected for one hundred years, but this protection and management is unique in the ten-thousand-plus years that humans have lived and roamed in southwest New Mexico. Prior to its establishment, the Gila Wilderness wasn't "wild," at least in the sense of how the word is often imagined. Native people relied on the forest for countless generations—they hunted elk, bears, beaver, and other animals; cut down trees for firewood and domicile construction; and cleared land for agriculture. Thus, the way the Gila Wilderness is presented to the public—a pristine place, devoid of human disturbance—is not reflective of its composition prior to European arrival, nor of how Native American ancestors used and appreciated it.

Every time I hike, camp, or pass through the Gila Wilderness, I think about its political or official establishment. While hiking its dry arroyos or scrambling along its cobbly escarpments, I'm as guilty as anyone of imagining myself in a primordial place that has been forever untrammeled and untamed. But I know this is a brief, historic anomaly. Native American ancestors were reliant on this land, and human impact here has ebbed and flowed over millennia. Native Americans would still be using and living in the Gila Wilderness were it not for their forced removal, which preceded the establishment of most national parks, forests, or monuments. In other words, white settlers are able to recreate in the Gila Wilderness because Native ancestors were forcibly removed from it. This seems particularly painful for the Gila, which served as a refuge for Apache people making a last stand against the intrusion of the US government. We need to ensure that this history is properly presented, and that Native American people are ensured access and use rights to these ancestral lands.

I'VE MADE DOZENS OF TRIPS to the Gila since that first winter more than ten years ago. In October 2013, the fall after the Silver Fire, I drove through the Black Range, now black, charred, and barren.

However, green shoots were starting to spring through—signs of resilience only four months after the conflagration.

My last trip was in August 2019. COVID-19 broke my streak of spending at least one day a year hiking or camping in the Gila, and I'm not sure when I'll be back. If I'm lucky, by the time this book is published, I'll have started a new streak with my daughter, who was born during the pandemic. I hope that the first time she visits, the Gila Wilderness will still be largely unchanged from when it was established a century ago. It will take much work and advocacy to ensure it remains unchanged by the time she reaches my age. Increasingly devastating fires seem likely. And while the Wilderness managed to survive one climate-change-denying, industry-friendly administration, I worry about similar administrations and their disregard for public lands.

We need places like the Gila Wilderness more than ever. We need places where people can escape and have visceral experiences that connect them to nature. We also need to learn from the people who resided in this area hundreds and thousands of years ago. To persist through challenging environmental times, modern society needs to be flexible. Rigid social institutions that are unwilling to adapt are likely to fail. If we are willing to modify how we interact with each other and the environment, we can persist through climate crises and continue to protect the Gila Wilderness for future generations.

PRISCILLA SOLIS YBARRA

THE IDEA OF WILDERNESS TO MEXICAN AMERICANS

ONE

F YOU ASK A MEXICAN AMERICAN, THEY WILL PROBABLY TELL
you that a place like the Gila Wilderness is not "wilderness"
at all. They would say that the land there is stolen.

The first person whose life will help tell this history is
Reies López Tijerina. For five days in October 1966, Tijerina and his group of activists, La Alianza, led a takeover of part
of the Carson National Forest in northern New Mexico. They
renamed it the Republic of San Joaquín del Rio de Chama, a ref-
erence to the 1806 Spanish grant that claimed the territory from
the original Apache, Ute, and Pueblo inhabitants. Tijerina's organization, whose full name was La Alianza Federal de Pueblos
Libres, included more than six thousand heirs, descendants of
the original recipients of fifty Mexican and Spanish land grants.
He was eventually arrested for the violation of public lands, but
not without first having his say.

In black-and-white archival footage of La Alianza's takeover,
Tijerina stands tall and dapper in a dark suit, his hair neatly
arranged with brilliantine in the same way that I remember my
father styling his. Tijerina speaks in the middle of a crowd of law
enforcement officials, explaining that La Alianza will take full
responsibility for the action. When a man wearing a badge tries
to cite a law to him, Tijerina interrupts, "Yes, I know your laws
already. We've been citizens of the United States for 120 years,
and we know the laws." Frustrated with being treated like a
second-class citizen, he references his in-depth studies of land
law, not only in the United States, but in Mexico and Spain as well.

La Alianza's aim was to restore the land to the Mexican American families dispossessed following the Mexican–American War, when Mexico lost half its territory to the United States. The 1848 Treaty of Guadalupe Hidalgo, which ended the war, also promised to make citizens of, and protect the property rights of, the approximately 110,000 Mexicans who chose to remain on lands annexed by the United States. But as with many US treaties, this one was not fully honored.

When I teach Chicanx Literature at the University of North Texas, I always start the class with a screening of the first episode of the four-part documentary film *Chicano! History of the Mexican-American Civil Rights Movement*. Part one, "Quest for a Homeland," begins with La Alianza's land takeover. Every semester, the students express frustration and disgust that they do not learn about the Mexican American civil rights movement until they are well into their college education. These students are by and large from Texas and educated in Texas public schools. I feel for them, too. I grew up in Texas and didn't learn about Chicanx history until I got to graduate school, first at UCLA and then at Rice.

The ideals of the US civil rights movement included transforming education so that such gaping holes of knowledge get filled. A part of that plan worked. Otherwise, this queer Chicana born in South Dallas would not be setting the curriculum in a college classroom. But so many of the contributions to US history from Black, Indigenous, Mexican American, Latinx, and Asian American communities still get left out. The overwhelming narrative that gets taught serves the delusion of white supremacy. The story of wilderness is no different. But the history of American conservation is not as white as we think it is.

TWO

TAKE ANOTHER EXAMPLE FROM NEW MEXICO: Estella Bergere Leopold. She was an American conservationist along with her

scientist-writer husband. Their five children also became leading scientists, academics, and conservationists; three have been
named to the National Academy of Sciences. But your typical
admirer of Aldo Leopold does not know the heritage of his wife
and children. Why does the Mexican American background of
one of the leading families of American conservation remain
hidden in plain sight?

Estella Bergere was born in Santa Fe, New Mexico, in 1890
to Eloisa Luna Bergere, a descendant of the Lunas, one of the
oldest settler families in the state, and Alfred M. Bergere, who
immigrated to the United States from Ireland. The Lunas trace
their lands back to the Spanish era, to the 1716 San Clemente
land grant that dispossessed Pueblo tribes in the area south
of present-day Albuquerque known as Los Lunas. The family
stayed on during the transition from Spanish colony to Mexican territory, and from Mexican territory to US territory and, in
1912, the state of New Mexico.

Aldo first arrived in the Southwest in 1909, freshly grad-
uated from the newly established Yale Forest School, to begin
as a ranger, first in Arizona territory and then in New Mexico
territory. He met and married Estella in 1912. Their eldest son,
Starker, was born in 1913, followed by brother Luna in 1915,
Adelina "Nina" in 1917, and Carl in 1919; the youngest, Estella,
was born in 1927, after the family moved to Madison, Wisconsin, where Aldo was professor of game management at the
University of Wisconsin. Even then, Estella and the kids spent
summers with their family back in Santa Fe.

In a sense, one might understand Aldo Leopold to be a
father of American wilderness. He went on to make an impact
in the areas of ecological restoration and environmental philosophy, too. But the wilderness movement in the Southwest
was built on lands acquired through the dispossession of many
Mexican American families of their property rights, which were
originally established by first displacing countless Indigenous

peoples from *their* relations with lands and sacred places. With this context in mind, what does it mean to be a father of American wilderness, anyway? When I say that the history of American conservation is not as white as we think it is, I want to draw attention to the Mexican American Leopolds as much as to emphasize that educators, environmentalists, conservationists, and activists need to make the ongoing violence of colonization visible when we tell the story.

Certainly, American conservation seems to mean well—establishing not just wilderness areas but national parks, monuments, forests, city parks, and protected beaches. But there's an insidious cover story going on here, that white Americans are the purveyors of this generosity. None of this so-called conservation would be possible without the original and ongoing dispossession and genocide of Indigenous peoples.

So when you ask a Mexican American about the wilderness and they tell you that it's stolen land, do they mean that it's stolen from Mexican Americans—or from our Indigenous relatives?

THREE

MEXICAN AMERICANS' MIXED IDENTITY INCLUDES our past as both colonizer and colonized. The third person who helps us understand the meaning of wilderness for Mexican Americans is Enriqueta Vásquez, a Chicana feminist writer and columnist for *El Grito del Norte*, the newspaper associated with Tijerina's land grant movement.

In the context of a movement that did not always make space for women's voices, Vásquez's column was titled "Despierten Hermanos!" (Wake Up, Brothers and Sisters!); her subject matter ranged from women's rights to cultural pride and environmental justice. Born in 1930 in southern Colorado, she grew up learning lessons of resilience from her family of migrant farmworkers. After surviving an abusive marriage and while taking care of her two children as a single mother on a secretary's salary, she crossed paths with Rodolfo "Corky" Gonzáles, the Chicano civil rights leader of the Crusade for Justice in Denver. Vásquez joined the movement and never looked back. When Gonzáles asked Vásquez and her second husband to move to northern New Mexico to help run a community school teaching Mexican American history and culture to children, she readily agreed.

In New Mexico, Vásquez became part of Tijerina's crusade for the land. But she and the staff of *El Grito*—which was comprised entirely of women—did not always agree with his approach. His goals involved repossession of the lands, while Vásquez and her *colegas* advocated for a position closer to that of Native nations to manage lands in a communal way. She urged readers to recall what Mexican Americans can learn from our Indigenous relations and our elders about how to care for the land. The Chicana writers of *El Grito* wanted hands off the land in the same ways that they wanted hands off their bodies. To these writer-activists, the liberation of women and of the land from colonization were one and the same.

In a December 7, 1970, column titled "La Santa Tierra," Vásquez wrote: "We learned from our *viejitos* of the balance of nature; that we should not kill birds, for they ate insects....That is a balance of nature; to know how all living things complement and harmonize with each other. That is how all things live from the earth." After commenting that those without a college education may in some ways be fortunate to escape "the Gringo value system," she also reasoned, "We can well understand why to a people who are capable of living in harmony with nature, it is very difficult to understand the concept of ownership and possession of land."

Vásquez did not learn this from scientists, conservationists, or white American writers like Leopold. The biggest insights, she argued, come from the peoples who embody survival and defiance: "If there is a whole truth," she wrote, "it must come from the people who have been able to endure for thousands of years." She urged the movement to "come home to our true selves, to our indigenous being, to our Indian family ties...alongside our Indian brothers and sisters, as a comrade nation." The Chicano Civil Rights Movement and the American Indian Movement, she advised, intersect on the land. "We go the way of the land; the way of the earth, the way of the water; the way of the wind," she wrote.

In the spring of 1970, in the column "Our New Nation is Born," Vásquez described a concept of land banks that had emerged at the second annual Chicano youth conference in Denver. There, conference participants set a political agenda for the movement. "Lands rightfully ours will be fought for and defended," Vásquez explained. "Land Banks will be set up immediately at the Crusade for Justice. Their purpose is to hold land communally by and for Chicanos." That idea of communalism is significant, as is the common cause against colonial violence across the globe, especially when the movement declared solidarity with political prisoners in Mexico and throughout Latin America.

Land banks, of course, differ greatly from the American concept of wilderness; their aim is to help liberate the land and the colonized peoples who care for it. Certainly, in the years that followed, they did not become a dominant land management practice. But the current #LandBack movement—as Indigenous land restoration is known today—is gaining momentum. In 2018, more than 17,000 acres were returned to the Cow Creek Band of Umpqua Tribe in western Oregon. In 2019, the City of Eureka, California, returned 200 acres to the Wiyot people. The Esselen Tribe purchased back 1,200 acres in Northern California in July 2020. And in 2021, over 18,000 acres of the National Bison Range and its resident bison herd were being restored to the Confederated Salish and Kootenai Tribes. I prefer the #LandBack vision to the alternative. American wilderness sits there with its soul hollowed out, emptied of the peoples who help animate the land.

WILDERNESS TO THE MEXICAN AMERICAN is stolen land. Whether it's stolen from Mexican Americans or stolen from Native nations will simply depend on who you ask. I join Enriqueta Vásquez in rallying Mexican Americans and Chicanxs to "come home to our true selves" to build coalitions with Native nations and advocate for #LandBack. It's what our ancestors would have wanted us to do. Because what's a land bank but another way of saying #LandBack?

HEAT 100

"I want to eat the dirt and lick the rock. Or leave the shade for the sun and feel the burning. I know I don't belong here. But this is the only place I belong."

—Charles Bowden
Inferno

BIRTHDAY FOR THE NEXT FOREST

Adapted from *A Song for the River*, 2018

BY SHEER DUMB LUCK I HAPPENED TO BE FACING THE lightning when it struck: a livid filament that reappeared on my eyelids when I blinked. A blue puff of smoke bloomed skyward from the top of the ridge, superheated sap boiled to vapor in an instant. It dispersed on the breeze so quickly I wondered whether I had imagined it—whether, having become at last clinically pyromaniacal, I had willed the tree to catch fire and conjured the evidence to prove it.

I reached for the field glasses where they hung from a hook in the ceiling of the fire tower, an instinctual move made without looking away from the spot of the strike. I lifted the binoculars to my eyes, focused on the ridgeline. Waited. Remembered to breathe. Waited some more. Nothing amiss. Nothing new or different along the contour of the hill.

Then it happened: the slightest rupture in the continuity of the view, a light white fog that ghosted the length of the tree and twisted through its branches, only to disperse again on the breeze. This smudge of smoke confirmed that I hadn't been hallucinating—that indeed a bolt from the clouds had lit the tree on fire, and I had been witness to the genesis. I set the binoculars aside, crouched behind the peephole of my Osborne Fire Finder, and waited for the smoke to puff again. When it did, I aimed the crosshairs through the viewfinder and noted the azimuth to the fraction of a degree.

This fact in hand, I turned to my maps and compared what they told me with the topography surrounding the smoke, noting its relation to the nearest prominent feature on the landscape, a small but unmistakable peak. Confident I had pinned the fire within a single square mile on the map, I called the dispatcher with my report: lightning-struck snag, narrow column of light-colored smoke, compass direction from me expressed in degrees azimuth, location by township, range, and section. The Silver Fire: named for nearby Silver Creek.

This one appeared poised to go big and stay awhile.

All the ingredients for a conflagration were in place. For the sake of cattle forage and stability on the watershed and a pleasing view of dense green trees from a tourist highway and a dozen other excuses that taken together amounted to outmoded and contradictory dogma, the surrounding country had been starved of fire—every new smoke suppressed as quickly as possible—going back a hundred years, an astonishing feat of military technology and human hubris. The result was an overgrown, unhealthy patch of forest further stressed by climate change. Thousands of dead white fir trees, killed by beetles a decade earlier, sprinkled the surrounding hillsides, and fuel moisture in the living trees had been sapped by years of substandard snowpack and above-average temperatures.

The weather forecast predicted the trifecta of hot, dry, windy conditions in the days ahead. All available smokejumpers had been dropped on two other fires earlier in the afternoon, so none were still on call for the initial attack. Despite being well outside the Wilderness, the topography was too steep and thickly forested for helicopter landings, so the only option for suppression was to send an engine crew whose members would have to hike cross country from the end of a bad dirt road, a trip that took four hours, drive time included.

For two full days I had a grandstand seat as my colleagues performed their suppression efforts—first the ground crew scratching a containment line, then air tankers dropping fire-retardant slurry. The containment line didn't hold because big conifers kept toppling and rolling downslope, starting new spot fires below the crew, who had no choice but to flee for their lives. I stayed in service with them past midnight that first night, scanning their radio traffic on the tactical channel, eavesdropping on their progress, and offering a communication link if they needed one, but I was of no use to their doomed efforts.

The next day's repeated slurry drops didn't hold because the fire had grown too hot, actively burning through the sundown hours when agency planes were forbidden to fly for safety reasons. They offered an impressive spectacle by daylight, two alternating bombers flying low over the ridge, first one, then the other, load-and-return from the aerial fire base all day long. The red-tinted mud unfurled in translucent streamers, dispersing into the treetops like a poison mist, but every drop of it—fifty thousand gallons of slurry, plus another thirty thousand of water—was for naught. It was one more run at the old game, putting out fires with emergency money in liquid form, but the rules of that game had been written in a previous century, under conditions that no longer applied.

On the fire's second night, I stood in the meadow on top of my mountain and watched the flames rupture the dark like lava spewing from a fissure in the earth. The slow-motion momentum of a natural catastrophe exerted a powerful spell: the sight menaced and titillated in equal measure. Even after I called out of service for the evening, I couldn't step away for more than half an hour before returning to the tower and staring some more. The fire had spread over seventy acres. The question now was whether the entire length of the Black Range would burn, or if some portion would be spared.

*

LATE IN THE MORNING of day three, a running crown fire took off in the canopy as the wind pushed the flames upslope toward the crest of the range. Two hundred acres burned in the span of an hour, trees torching like Roman candles in flame lengths of one hundred feet. Mesmerized, I watched the smoke—first white, then darkening through various shades of gray, finally culminating in black—rise skyward like the plume from a muddy geyser.

The order to evacuate came just after lunch. I was told I had forty-five minutes to grab the possessions dearest to me and lock up the facilities for a departure of indefinite duration. A helicopter would soon spool up to pluck me from the peak and deliver me to the trailhead, where my truck was parked directly in the path of the fire.

I hauled my gear out to the Marston Mat helipad—typewriter, box of books, backpack full of clothes, cooler of perishable food, a few other odds and ends—and made one last walk around the mountain, noting the various man-made flammables. Among them were the aspenwood hitching post I had just rebuilt, the picket fence around the propane tanks, the sign welcoming visitors, the old log cabin. Whether any or all would remain when I returned was an open question.

Oblivious to the drama playing out five miles south, hummingbirds clustered at the feeders I had hung for them. They drank my simple-syrup mixture, chittering and whistling, flaring their wings to mime dominance or dislodge a seat at the table. The syrup would be gone in a day or two without me around to replenish it—but the fire would force the birds to find new feeding grounds anyway. They would move on. They would survive.

Soon the distant buzz of the chopper made itself heard, a low percussive hum that gathered strength until it roared over the meadow. The grass bent beneath the force of the rotor like seaweed swaying in the tide. Two helitack personnel ducked out the side door and loaded my supplies, a perfunctory job, performed wordlessly. It was a humbling and even sort of sickening feeling to board the machine for the flight out. More than a hundred times I had come and gone from the mountain over the years, mostly under power of my own two legs, a few times by the legs of a horse. To leave by the magic of internal combustion was as dispiriting as it was novel, almost equal parts elation and despair, with a side helping of guilt given my devotion to nonmotorized Wilderness travel. The point of the work is early detection: the sooner you spot a fire, the more options you give firefighters to manage it. When you're airlifted by the whirlybird, their options have dwindled—and so have yours—to none but run.

Over the course of eleven summers, I had sat in my mountain minaret and marveled at the harshness and beauty of the view, but to see it for the first time from a bird's perspective astonished me anew. As the chopper rumbled along the crest toward the trailhead, I looked out the window upon a forbidding landscape, east-west canyons dropping sharply from the top of the divide, each of them cradled by shark-fin ridges and brutal bluffs—a forest of Douglas fir and white pine on the high peaks, pockets of aspen on the north-facing slopes, ponderosa on the south aspects, here and there a piñon pine. The smooth white bark of certain aspens still showed cowboy dendroglyphs carved almost a century ago. Amid them stood gnarly survivor trees whose bark had been corkscrewed by lightning. Others were marked by the scars of old ground fires at their base. A few of them had been almost like friends to me, sources of wonder and comfort. Their cool breath. Their proud bearing. Their highly individual shapes. Being among the most rooted of life forms— challenged by changing climatic conditions, unable to flee more immediate catastrophes—they were uniquely vulnerable organisms, which only added to their beauty. I tried to fix them in my imagination even as I bid them goodbye.

When we landed at the pass, I stepped from the chopper and removed my flight helmet to watch the smoke rise and spin like a cyclone to the south, a vortex of unimaginable heat. Ash fell like flakes of snow on the hood of my pickup truck, and the growl of the fire could be heard more than a mile away.

I joined the Black Range district ranger and three firefighters standing on the edge of the paved overlook, none of us quite capable of articulating the awe we felt at what we saw and what it meant for a forest we knew well and loved. I reminded myself that the mountains had always known fire, were in fact born in a cataclysm of fire, during a great volcanic explosion in the Eocene Epoch, an event orders of magnitude more dazzling than even the most spectacular wildfire. Created in fire, the mountains would naturally succumb to it for renewal and rebirth.

June 7, 2013, happened to be the day they did so.

WHEN ITS GROWTH CEASED, four weeks after it began, the Silver Fire had moved across 138,705 acres, or 214 square miles.

My boss granted me permission to return to my mountain in the final week of July. "Don't get too depressed up there," he said. "Remember, a big fire is just the birthday for the next forest. It will be green again before long."

It was a peculiar hike in, that first time back. Much of the walk was lacking in living vegetation. It felt spooky to be so exposed in a place where the forest had once provided the shade of an intermittent canopy. Now there was no proper canopy, just a bare etching of black branches against a pale blue sky. On a trail I had hiked so often I could make my way along it in the dark, I felt as if I were having the inverse of a déjà vu experience—traveling through a familiar place made newly strange.

The view to the south, where the fire first got up and ran, encompassed a stunning tableau of destruction, a ten-thousand-acre patch of forest transformed into charcoal: a century of accumulated biomass reduced to blackened stalks overnight. It had the naked look of country whose soil structure might unravel with one hard rain. But three-quarters of the way to the top, big stands of intact forest appeared where the fire didn't climb into the crowns of the trees, thanks to a mid-June rain that moderated fire behavior for a weekend. That pause helped preserve my immediate environs far better than I had dared hope, in part by allowing a window of opportunity for a burnout operation. With the smoke and flames tamped down by higher humidity, a helicopter was able to maneuver in close enough to drop ping-pong balls juiced with potassium permanganate and glycol in a big circle around the lookout. When the balls hit the ground, they ignited the surface fine fuels but spared the trees above, robbing the Silver Fire of continuous fuel—fire fought with fire. Standing in the middle of the open meadow on the mountain, rejoicing in the sight of the cabin and tower standing unscathed, I could hardly tell there had been a burn in the neighborhood at all. The peak still wore its cap of pine and fir, and the meadow grasses were luxuriant from the rains.

As I made my initial survey of the facilities, something caught my eye in the grass, something bright green and gently quivering. I bent close and studied it: a mountain tree frog. I had heard its telltale croak on occasion, late in previous seasons, usually around the pond on the flank of the mountain, but I had never seen one up on top. I sat down near it, as unthreateningly as possible, and tried to remain as still as it did for the next half hour, my compatriot on an island of green, each of us breathing but otherwise motionless.

It thrilled me as much as any wildlife encounter I had ever experienced—it contrasted so starkly with my pessimistic assumptions of what I would find on my return. Despite a decade of visiting the aftermath of big burns, seeing how quickly the regrowth came, I had arrived expecting only the funereal this time, probably because the changes hit extra close to home. My attachment to the landscape surrounding that mountain had arisen from an ongoing intimacy with all its moods and weathers and creatures. It had been cemented by a fondness for certain special places I had come to think of as sacred, places whose beauty had offered me a lifeline through more than one kind of loss: in the beginning, the death of a brother; more recently, the end of a marriage. With the forest reshaped, I had feared another in a suite of losses whose accumulated weight I struggled to bear.

Many of us who lived in and cared about the American West felt that sense of mounting loss, felt it in our physical beings— our reason for living here rooted in the physical, after all, both the land's and our own. We liked the look and feel and smell of the mountains, and we liked to test ourselves in them, hiking, skiing, rock climbing, horseback riding, fly fishing, elk hunting—you name it, there was something for everyone, and big chunks of public land on which to do it. But landscapes we loved were being transformed on a scale that was hard to absorb; entire mountain ranges were burning up. For a hundred years we mostly kept the scorch at bay. And just as we awoke to the rude fact of our mistake, the fires became bigger and more intense than any we had ever seen, even in places like the Gila, with a decades-long history of aggressive burning, though not quite aggressive enough. Scorched earth was now the ground we inhabited in the forests of the American West.

IN THE ESSAY "Lifetimes with Fire," Gary Snyder wrote:

> In 1952 and '53 I worked on fire lookouts in the Skagit District of the Mount Baker forest, northern Washington Cascades. Crater Mountain first and then Sourdough. Those were the first jobs I'd held that I felt had some virtue. Guarding against forest fires, finally I had found Right Occupation. I congratulated myself as I stood up there above the clouds memorizing various peaks and watersheds, for finding a job that didn't contribute to

the Cold War and the wasteful modern economy. The joke's on me as I learn fifty years later how much the fire suppression ideology was wrong-headed and how much it has contributed to our current problems.

I knew that feeling of self-congratulation. I had once bailed on a career in corporate journalism because I came to detest its narrow range of acceptable opinion and its attitude of deference to officially constituted power. I ran away to a lookout tower in the world's first Wilderness and even managed by sheer happenstance to land in a place with an enlightened attitude about fire. I bathed in my sense of good fortune and felt a little smug every time I thought of my friends toiling away at their computers back east, feeding the bottomless maws of the content machines. But the joke was on me. I had arrived seeking freedom and found more than my fair share, the nearest thing on earth to my own private utopia. The price was my attendance at what came to feel like a wake for the Holocene.

In the southern Black Range, the old, green forest lived only in remnants and memories, and some of the memories were mine. It was a sobering thought, the idea that my mind, if I lived another forty years, might become one of the last repositories on earth of how certain stands of old growth looked and felt and smelled in a place once called "the wildest Wilderness in the West." At first, I wondered whether the fire would deform my connection with the country—whether it would inflict a wound that would forever disfigure my passion for it. Instead, I found I loved it more than ever, indeed felt an obligation to continue my annual mountain-sitting retreat for as long as I felt physically able, years into the future I dared hope, in order to see what the place would become, what capability for resilience it possessed, if only we could leave it the hell alone and let it burn.

SHARMAN APT RUSSELL

A STONE IN OUR POCKET

WILDERNESS BURNS. A FEW MILES FROM MY HOME in southwestern New Mexico, nearly three hundred thousand acres of the Gila National Forest and Gila Wilderness burned in the 2012 Whitewater-Baldy Fire. It was the largest in the state's history. Across the American West, other wildernesses have burned in the recent past, and more will burn in the future, stands of beetle-infested trees ignited by dry winters and dry springs and a summer spark, fires fueled by decades of fire suppression in forests adapted to regular, low-intensity burns. After the 2012 fire, in a pilgrimage westerners know well, I returned to hike trails once so familiar. I turned in a circle. A dark circle of ship masts. In a hard wind, years later, they would become a giant game of pick-up sticks. A game stretching to the horizon.

The burned spruce in the Gila Wilderness won't return, not for thousands of years. Instead, aspen are growing, dog-hair thick, taller every day. Overnight, a ponderosa pine forest shifts to scrub brush like New Mexican locust and Gambel oak. Wilderness burns. Wildness remains. As climate change sweeps like a broom over the places we love, gathering spruce and fir into a refuse pile, brushing up species like spotted owls and leopard frogs, as we see entire landscapes wither and char, wildness remains—in particular, the wildness honored, promised, protected, managed, betrayed, and adored in the American wilderness system.

On the banks of the Gila River, I crouch low and readjust my close-focusing binoculars. I am watching a western red-bellied tiger beetle lift up on its long legs—stilting—in a display of thermoregulation, getting a fraction farther away from the heat of the sand. Tiger beetles are among the fastest and fiercest insects in the world—one species can gallop five miles an hour—with large protruding eyes and heavy mandibles that they scissor like a chef sharpening his knives. Spotting a spider or ant, these hunters run after their prey, grab, stab, dismember, drench the victim in digestive juices, and suck up the puree with a straw-like mouthpart. Tiger beetle larvae are equally predacious. After hatching from tiny eggs, the tiny grubs use tiny jaws to dig a vertical tunnel. Two hooks on their backs anchor them firmly inside the burrow, and from this position they lunge out like B-movie monsters, catching even smaller insects. Eventually the larvae pupate into adults. Thousands of western red-bellied adults swarm this riverbank where I crouch and watch, their heads and thoraxes iridescent in the sun, their wing covers brown with six creamy dots. Each beetle is only a third of an inch long. I'm glad for that.

Here in New Mexico, environmentalists have spent years preventing a diversion on the Gila River, the Southwest's last free-flowing river. They keep in check the ambitions of an international mining company, which owns the majority of water rights in the Gila Valley. They advocate for regulation of ATVs in the national forest. They lobby for new wilderness. They go to meetings with county commissioners and local agencies. They drive up to Santa Fe for meetings. They meet with each other. These environmentalists don't have much free time to spend in the Gila Wilderness, which remains what designated wilderness was meant to be: a place to visit and hold in your mind. A touchstone. A stone from the river.

The grasshopper mouse creeps from her burrow in the crepuscular evening or under the buttery moonlight or glitter of stars, hoping for a scorpion. Finding one, she rushes and pounces, front paws extended. The scorpion lashes. The mouse leaps up. The scorpion stings. The mouse tries to bite off that stinging tail. Lashing, biting, stinging, leaping. In picoseconds now—trillionths of seconds—proteins in the mouse's nerve cells are binding with the scorpion venom and blocking the pain signal. More lashing, more biting, more stinging, more leaping. After the struggle, or perhaps before, the mouse lifts her head in the iconic pose of a wolf howling, and then she does howl, a high-pitched screech and celebratory exult: this is my scorpion. She may also howl as a territorial warning: this is my land, and not just a pocket mouse kind of land, but as much as twenty-five acres, all mine. Sometimes a male will howl, too, as a love song, although love is edgy since partners occasionally kill each other. Every day is edgy for grasshopper mice, who range from Mexico to Canada, living in harsh, arid places, getting all or most of their water from meat. This seems to be working well for them. Grasshopper mice seen in four-million-year-old fossils look much like grasshopper mice today.

In the burned areas of ponderosa pine forest, many of the big trees will recover. Now in the spring, large thickets of New Mexican locust also burst out with masses of fleshy pink and purple blossoms, luxuriant clumps clearly in the pea family, and I think suddenly that I am in a garden, not the Gila Wilderness. But this is not a garden meant for me, a big two-footed animal, on a stroll. This locust, for example, has a pair of stiff, stout, curved thorns at the base of its leaves. Intellectually, I know that thorns protect a plant from being eaten by herbivores. Take that, cow! And deer. And Pleistocene camel. Having lived almost all my life in the Southwest, I know thorns. It's not a hate/love relationship. I just hate the way catclaw acacia rakes my skin, needle sharp. I dislike the jab of a prickly pear on my ankle. I rightly fear tumbling down a slope and jamming my knee into a cholla cactus. Still, the locust flowers smell deliciously sweet, and I put some of this glory in my backpack, remembering that Apache people ate these blossoms raw or in stews. I'll try that, too, mixed with spinach and arugula. (Other parts of the tree, of course, are toxic.) In the coming years, I'll be seeing more plants like the New Mexican locust, with strong underground root systems that sprout soon after a forest fire. Likely, these plants will also have thorns.

As a nature writer, I've promised myself again and again not to bring up the hoary figures of Henry David Thoreau and Ralph Waldo Emerson and John Muir. Enough with those guys. We need the voices of the twenty-first century now, not the nineteenth. Still, I can't help but mention here a common misquote. Thoreau didn't say, "In wilderness is the preservation of the world," as some people seem to think. He said, in *wildness*. In wildness is the preservation of the world. And now we ask ourselves in this rapidly changing world—what is the meaning of wild? What will preserve us?

Like other people who live with fire, I change my hiking routine. The Gila National Forest is three million acres. There are many trails here, through juniper and hackberry, across fields of grama grass. Near the Gila River, a coati—relative of the raccoon but not a raccoon—watches me from the branches of a cottonwood. Dark eyes, masked face. A long white nose. And that thick beautiful red-gold coat with banded tail gold and brown. What a decorative animal. Confident and curious. Perhaps twenty pounds but seemingly bigger. "Hey, beautiful," I say. I suspect this coati to be a bachelor male, having left the matriarchal family group, all those bossy moms and aunties and dominant female leader, everyone always talking to each other—chittering, churring, barking. This coati is not alarmed that I am talking to him, too—that I always talk to the coatis I meet. That something in my chest blooms, an effervescent excitement, giddy and yearning at the same time.

For decades, coatis have been expanding their range up from the tropics and through the deserts of Mexico and New Mexico, establishing themselves in the changing forests where I live. In the language of coatis, *churr* means "sweetling." *Ha-ha-ha* is a warning. A *bark* is a laugh. In the language of fire, a Gambel oak has a root system that goes ten feet down and weighs two hundred pounds. A stand of aspen are a single organism; every tree rises from the same root. In the language of scorpions, the nerve cells of a grasshopper mouse open to receive venom. Suddenly, proteins enfold that chemical in unexpected embrace. More openings, more closing. All this happens on a scale of matter and time that leaves us dizzy, disordered.

Wild landscapes seen and unseen. Wild landscapes carried home, put in a salad. So we learn to live in this world. So we carry the Gila Wilderness, a stone in our pocket. So we talk to ourselves and the animals and plants we meet: Hello, aren't you beautiful?

FIRE BIRD

THE BIRD FLEW ACROSS SIGNAL PEAK ROAD WITH THE distinct undulations of a woodpecker—a graceful glide on the downbeat, rhythmic wingbeats on the upstroke. It had launched from the long shadows of the scorched skeletons of trees on the right-hand side of the road. The bird settled on a tree to my left, its dark body almost impossible to see against the charred black bark. As suddenly as it appeared, it returned to the other side of the road. In its flight I saw the smoky black of its shoulders, the smudged white on its back. It was an American three-toed woodpecker, a bird I had only seen in field guides.

A topo map showed that I was standing at an elevation of about 7,500 feet. I was surrounded by the vestiges of the Signal Fire, a "human-caused fire with an undetermined ignition source," according to the official statement from the US Forest Service. The Signal Fire burned 5,740 acres before it was suppressed. Perhaps a camper got careless with a cooking fire. Perhaps a celebration at a family picnic got out of hand. Whatever the cause, someone holding a lighter or a lit match didn't seriously consider the danger in a forest in the middle of a megadrought. The fire started on an especially windy Mother's Day in 2014; two years and two months later, I could still smell the smoke.

I tiptoed into the gloom of the standing snags to get closer to the bird. It was hard to imagine the vibrant green life that once thrived here. Signal Peak Road is a fire-lookout access road that climbs to nine thousand feet, through an area once thick with ponderosa pines. The fire had created a somber atmosphere but allowed me my first glimpse of this woodpecker, an opportunistic bird that survives amid devastation.

New Mexico had experienced record-setting fire seasons during two of the three years before the Signal Fire, and some of those fires were here in the Gila National Forest. In 2012, lightning sparked two separate fires in the Mogollon Mountains east of Glenwood. When they converged, the combined White-water-Baldy Fire raced across almost three hundred thousand acres—bigger than the land area of San Antonio, Texas, and roughly the size of the city of Los Angeles—to become the largest fire in New Mexico history. And the drought continues.

Although there is no legal definition of drought, we all know it means there is not enough water. The US Drought Monitor began recording precipitation totals around the country in 2000 and comparing this data to long-term averages. The findings show that the longest-lasting drought in New Mexico began in May 2001 and ended in August 2007. In January 2021, exceptional drought—meaning migratory birds changed their flight patterns and no surface water was available for agriculture—was affecting more than half of all land in New Mexico. Some experts predict that the extended drought experienced here in the early 2000s will be the norm by the middle of this century.

Three-toed woodpeckers prefer trees eighty years old and older, which, unlike the birds themselves, are easy to find in the Gila. Stands of smaller trees that were not logged or burned in the 1930s still exist, although in the Gila, a hundred-year-old tree might still be skinny enough for you to wrap your arms around. I had read that the best way to find three-toed woodpeckers—as well as the bark beetles they favor—is to look for bits of bark at the base of burned trunks. Fallen bark bits were hard to spot among the red-brown pine needles and charred twigs that littered the ground. As I listened, the woodpecker started a slow drumming that fell off in pace and intensity at the end of her phrase. Then she began flicking off pieces of bark from a scorched trunk and letting them drop; I watched them pile up at the base of the tree.

My *Sibley Guide to Birds* told me that American three-toed woodpeckers are uncommon Gila residents. Smaller than robins and most other woodpeckers, they have short tails and rather large heads. They are mostly dark with dense barring across their backs and breasts, making them hard to distinguish from the charcoal trunks they climb searching for grubs. My bird resembled other types of woodpeckers I was familiar with in the area—ladder-backs, hairys—but was also distinctive. With none of the yellowish speckles that males have on their crowns, I was certain I was seeing a female.

I held my binoculars steady to get a better look at a bird described as "quiet and elusive." With three toes on each foot—two forward and one back—they are unique among other species of woodpeckers, the four-toed types. Having three toes makes them especially adept at digging beetles out from under the superficial layers of tree bark, but this evolutionary adaption demands a price: three-toed woodpeckers spend more energy climbing tree trunks than other woodpeckers. I watched the female grab some beetles before climbing a few inches and stripping off another section of bark.

LIKE MANY FORESTS ACROSS the American West, the Gila National Forest has experienced heavy bark beetle outbreaks. There are about six hundred species of bark beetles in the United States; as a group, these insects, the size of rice grains, have destroyed millions of acres of trees distressed by drought and above average temperatures. Bark beetles, the favorite meal of three-toed woodpeckers, lay their eggs under the surface layers of bark in tunnels called *galleries*. After a summer or two, depending on the species, the beetles morph from larvae to pupae and finally emerge as adults. They spend winters beneath the bark, protected from snow and ice. A three-toed woodpecker searches for these young and adult beetles by peeling away the outer layers of bark, flinging its head from side to side and exposing the galleries. If you look closely, you can see the marks scored by their bills in the wood. It is said that in severely infected forests, you can hear the beetles chewing their way through the living tree tissue. The woodpeckers hear it, too. Approximately 65 percent of a three-toed woodpecker's yearly diet consists of bark beetles; in winter, that figure climbs to 99 percent.

If you have driven through any forested mountain range in the American West, you have seen the devastation caused by these bugs. My visit to Signal Peak Road happened to be during the peak of the beetle-caused tree mortality in the Gila that lasted from 2015 to 2018. From where I stood, looking at the ghosts of ponderosa pines, I assumed that fire was responsible for the majority of destruction of western forests. But people who study these things for a living have told me that, annually, bark beetles damage more acres of forest than the total area damaged by fire.

Even after a fire, bark beetles need living trees to survive. Trees not completely consumed by fire still contain enough living tissue for the beetles to eat, which in turn means breakfast, lunch, and dinner for three-toed woodpeckers. The one I was watching on Signal Peak Road had followed beetles that probably arrived at the scene a couple of weeks after the fire had been contained. The beetles and the woodpeckers spend about two years eating all they can glean from a stand of trees, until the trees have nothing more to offer the beetles and, eventually, the woodpeckers.

Bark beetles are considered by some to be the scourge of western forests, but in forests undisturbed by fire or drought, they can actually contribute to the health of a forest by helping to recycle decomposing wood. The problem is that increasingly more forests in the West are experiencing larger, more extreme fires and drought. The only sure beetle-control method would be an extremely long, extremely cold spell that would kill the over-wintering larvae. But winters have become too warm, allowing some species of beetles to erupt at elevations and latitudes where winters used to be too frigid for their larvae to survive.

Some forest ecologists believe three-toed woodpeckers could provide a solution. By peeling away bark and exposing beetle larvae to freezing temperatures, woodpeckers help keep populations in check. Conservation groups point out that the USDA policy of allowing beetle-infested trees to stand benefits three-toed woodpecker populations, which in turn helps limit beetle outbreaks. This is especially helpful in forests like the Gila, where the woodpeckers live year-round.

I felt fortunate to see this bird. American three-toed wood-peckers are considered a sensitive species, defined by ornitholo-gist David Wiggins as a population whose "current or predicted downward trends in density or habitat capability will reduce its distribution." The Gila lies at the extreme southern end of their range, which extends into Alaska and across Canada. As the cli-mate crisis continues, forests will begin to recede north, pushing the woodpeckers' range further out of New Mexico and Colo-rado. Continued drought and warming temperatures could even drive the species to extinction.

I RETURNED TO SIGNAL PEAK Road in February 2021 to try to get another look at a three-toed woodpecker. I had to delay my trip for a week after a winter storm dropped heavy snow across most of New Mexico. The moisture was welcome but just a drop in the proverbial bucket; by February, the exceptional drought that began to creep across the state at the end of 2020 had extended its range across the southern New Mexico border to El Paso and beyond. By the time I arrived, Highway 15 was dry leading out of Silver City and well plowed in the mountains in the national forest. I turned off the highway onto a slushy Signal Peak Road that only got messier. After my car fishtailed for about a quarter mile, I figured getting stuck in the snow on a sparsely traveled mountain road was probably not a good idea. I was not going to get a second look at a three-toed woodpecker. I would not have my breath taken away by the dramatic vistas of the Gila Wilderness from the summit. I would not even reach the Signal Fire burn scar to look for signs of new growth among the destruction caused by the fire. I drove in reverse all the way back to the parking lot off Highway 15. I stood in the snow and watched two male hairy woodpeckers chasing a female through healthy ponderosa pines under a bright blue sky.

On the drive back to Silver City, I stopped at a pullout to catch sight of the distant land I could not reach. Looking over the Continental Divide, I imagined how different this view would be after five more years, or ten, or fifty. In the long term, not all changes will be negative, of course, although the environmental, spiritual, and economic impacts of the loss of forests will be impossible to measure. I asked myself how much change I am able to accept, and how much choice I will have regarding what's coming.

The wilderness area visible to the northeast from the overlook where I stood is named after the man who said that our challenge was "building receptivity into the still unlovely human mind." Aldo Leopold also said, "There must be some force behind conservation more universal than profit...something that reaches into all times and places....I can see only one such force: a respect for land as an organism; a voluntary decency in land-use exercised by every citizen and every land-owner out of a sense of love for and obligation to that great biota we call America."

The climate crisis asks how each of us can practice decency in our interactions with the four classic elements of our physical world—fire, water, earth, and air. Approaches to fire management have evolved over time, from total suppression to "light burning" to emergency action only. Complex water policies in the West seem to agree only on the fact that our available tools inadequately address the challenges posed by too little water. Air-quality standards and sustainable land-use policies are slow to adapt to a changing climate. How much management is too much? How much hubris is involved in thinking we are in control at all?

Different species will replace the trees lost to fires and bark beetles, and three-toed woodpeckers will move further north in response to the changes in their range. But how will we adapt?

MICHAEL P. BERMAN

LEARNING TO FALL

F YOU WANT TO FIND A WILD PLACE, LEAVE BEHIND YOUR MAPS, your compasses, and your homing devices that tell you how to stay safe. A wild place distinguished by a boundary on a map is without the intimacy of breath, or the breadth of perspective. It is a category of separation. What is wild to us is simply the world of every other living thing on this planet.

The Gila is big enough that I may just be ignorant of what is out there. I may just get lost. Still, I am most comfortable when I hike alone, without a proper plan, without a marked trail, and without having left behind a date for my return. Such behavior teaches me to pay attention. Sometimes folks admonish me and ask, "But what would happen if you fell?"

The question always makes me a little bit sad. When I kicked around the Mongolian Gobi Desert, trying to figure out how to get to the closed areas along the Chinese border, my driver had learned the English word "dangerous." He used it every time he did not want to go somewhere. I learned to reply with the Mongolian word *sonirkoltoi*, which means "interesting." A world in which you never fall is not very interesting.

The Gila is a caldera, but rather than a single cone rising above the horizon, it is a mega caldera, a circle of two hundred miles of old volcanoes and mountain ranges. The three forks of the Gila River drain the central basin. Like Yellowstone, its sister to the north, this natural fortress protects a complex of diverse ecological systems. On a satellite map, the surface reticulates in a thousand canyons like the dried skin of old elephant hide, and forests stretch for miles and take on the names of trees: piñon-juniper, Douglas fir, and cathedral halls of giant yellow ponderosa pines.

I have never met anyone along the trails that climb up out of the San Francisco River valley to the top of the Mogollon Mountains. The Mogollons are big, but they are not spectacular, and this is their saving grace. I imagine most folks look at a map, drive around on the Bursum Road, and hike the Hummingbird Saddle Trail if they want to reach the high peaks.

This dry country is all about rain, because there is never enough of it. My Mexican friends on the ranches in Chihuahua, our neighbors to the south, have a saying: *Lluvias de mayo, ni maíz pal caballo.* Rain in May, no corn for the horses. What they mean is that in a good year springtime is dry and early summer is drier, until the celebratory bang of thunder and lightning on or about the Fourth of July that marks the return of the summer monsoons. Our best storms push giant thunderheads above the Mogollons. And so, on a late June afternoon, I started up Little Dry Creek hoping to get into the high country before the rain.

Little Dry is a stream with pools that, though they are not big enough to swim in, are deep enough to lie down in on a hot day. It is swaddled in three wooded folds: a sycamore-beech-alder-ash-cottonwood riparian bottom with piñon-juniper-oak-manzanita Madrean woodland on one side and ponderosa-fir forest on the other, all part of the intersection of ecosystems that makes the Gila special. I raced up the bottom, filling my canteen before the trail swung up and out of the canyon towards Windy Gap, a little saddle behind a promontory knob. I was inattentive to the ground under my feet as I anticipated a panoramic sunset on the cliffs above, and for the first time, I fell.

I tripped. Not a half-kick of a stone, or a stumble on a root, but my own personal ballet. I caught a stick on the toe of my boot, the one following behind, and when it slid into the crook of my ankle as my back leg moved forward, I went down like a heeled and dallied calf. The trick when you trip is not to stick your arm out, not to risk a broken wrist. Instead, flop on your belly, or make a slight turn so you hit the ground on your side in a fetal curl. A quick survey: nothing broken. I went on.

AT WINDY GAP, A WEATHERED brown Forest Service sign tells you there is no trail into the next canyon over. These are my favorite government signs, and this one marks my favorite trail in the Gila: a barely navigable track into what folks in the West call "rough country," down to a beautiful trout stream called Dry Creek. The place has not been saved by our good intentions—there is an abandoned mine cabin in the lower canyon and the old trail attests to our effort to bring it under dominion. But it is just too damn hard to get at. And that might be the proper definition of our wildernesses: places too damn hard for people to get at.

It was too late and too dark, so instead of going into Dry Creek that night I stayed on the people trail and headed up Sacaton Mountain. The trail straddles the ridge between Big and Little Dry, traversing stepped rhyolite cliffs under an open sky. On an evening with clean air, and I mean really clean air from LA to El Paso, at dusk, when the first stars appear, the stratosphere catches the rays from the sun, now well below the horizon, and lights up the world in a rose-colored glow. People who know this light, and the dance with glee that it conjures, may still believe fairies and gremlins live in these woods.

I was up over the hump and into Simmons Saddle when I crashed to earth for the second time. I slipped on a brown pancake that turned to green slime as soon as my foot came down. I had stepped in shit—a cow pie. One of the charms of wilderness in the West is cows.

A slip is not a trip. You slip when you step on a layer of soft on top of something hard, in my case, slimy shit on firm ground.

When you slip, instead of your momentum throwing you forward, you have a more indeterminate fate, a tendency to overcompensate and throw yourself back. Your feet come out from under you and down you go on your ass.

My advice might be counterintuitive. Go with the fall and get to the ground. If you fight the slip and try to stay on your feet, you increase the momentum with which you ultimately hit the ground and risk a wrenched back or twisted knee. More often, folks get hurt when they fight the fall. Best when something goes wrong or you make a mistake to admit it and move on. My canteen was dry and I stopped at Simmons Saddle Spring. There was only mud and a lot more cow shit. Time to move on.

Section4(d)(4)(2) of the Wilderness Act states: *The grazing of livestock, where established prior to the effective date of this Act, shall be permitted to continue subject to such reasonable regulations as are deemed necessary by the Secretary of Agriculture.*

In 1984, the Forest Service wrote a Memorandum of Understanding for a young third-generation rancher. The document said, go ahead, buy the Diamond Bar, the largest cattle allotment in the wilderness, and we'll let you bring in a D-9 bulldozer, *and* you can put in as many stock ponds as you want, *and*—in a display of the magical thinking that says you can fix the damage cows do by running more cows—you can triple the number of cattle.

This math did not work out very well. The streams on the Diamond Bar had already been stripped of riparian vegetation, and bare uplands shed water and soil. The people who live here had to endure a painful ten-year argument over those stock ponds and grazing allotments.

The resolution was rather remarkable. Cows were removed from the Diamond Bar, and the Forest Service enforced some of the grazing regulations. Quite a few of the allotments were shown to be unsuitable for grazing. I have a map, "Livestock Occurrence and Inventory Status and Perennial Streams Gila

National Forest—June 19, 2002," which shows a little over a third of the Gila National Forest was closed to grazing. It also shows that you can have both grazing and wilderness in a national forest. Just not in the same place.

But the pressure to develop resources continues, and over time the enviros decided it was easier and more profitable to avoid the issue, and almost all the forest once again has cows, whether on re-permitted allotments or with trespass cattle. If you want wilderness, wild places, and healthy ecosystems; if you want timber, water, and cattle—we need to have a conversation about what is on the table.

CONSERVATION PROJECTS FOCUS ON the things we can see, and a spectacular view with a couple geological anomalies is important for a campaign to save a place. I am a photographer, and I photograph these anomalies. I also photograph the vast swaths of lands folks call barren and empty, because I have this quixotic vision that these are the places that tie the world together. An image is defined by shadow and perspective. Objects have a dark and a light side and shrink in scale as they merge beneath the horizon.

At night what we see is no longer so solid. Vistas are empty and the scale of the horizon can be a few feet or many miles away. At night what is spectacular merges with the subtle and envelops us within the small threads of the web of life and the infinity of the sky. The Gila has very dark skies.

I love to walk at night. Under the velvet sheen of the Milky Way, it is bright even on a moonless night, and this night had a quarter moon heading to the horizon. As the moon set, the ridge took on the surreal look of an archipelago as I coursed along the edge of black vistas.

When you walk at night, it is about balance and moving between what you see and what is there. The center of the eye has the least sensitive vision in the dark, so try not to focus on every little thing. Instead use your eyes for an idea of the way forward and feel the ground beneath your feet. The health of an ecosystem is manifest in softness of the soil. Game trails are subtle and have a dendritic flow between water, food, and shelter; our forged trails are hard underfoot and cut through the land from Point A to Point B. You will feel the world change when you leave a marked trail.

I was thinking about water when I saw a campfire up ahead. It disappeared and reappeared. I got curious and thought I might find something to drink and some conversation. Then it disappeared again, and I thought, *What the hell* is *that?* It reappeared, and I saw that what I had thought was a campfire in the near distance was in fact lines of wildfire moving across the mountains a few miles below me.

In the 1990s, the Gila National Forest was known for its progressive forest fire policy. While every other forest worked hard at putting out every fire they could, the Gila let a few burn—about 5 percent. It gave us a glimpse of how forest and fire are something that go together.

Folks still thought they could manage wildfire now and forever. Notice the words "manage" and "wild." They do not go together. Sooner or later, it is one or the other. Fire management, timber management, and grazing management shifted the ecology of the Gila. We cut the fire-resistant trees and encouraged cattle to strip the fine fuels that burn the understory quickly. The land got more and more choked up with brush that burned the understory hot and jumped into the canopy.

We got very good at putting out the small fires the forest needed, but with the extremes of dry summers, the fires we could not put out got larger. The Forest Service fought the fires like a war, until they lost. In 2012, the Whitewater-Baldy megafire wiped out most of the big trees.

I WAS THIRSTY WHEN I reached Spruce Creek Saddle. I never run out of water in the desert. It is a categorical of life. In the mountains I think, *Why should I have to carry water up when streams and springs send it down?* I should know better. In late June you cannot depend even on the springs marked on the maps. But I figured I'd get up with the sun. If you work your way into the woods, there is always water at the headwaters. I threw down a sleeping bag, rolled out my pad, and went to sleep.

The wind woke me up. I opened one eye and then the other in the way you do when you are exhausted, still into only an hour or so of sleep. The world was filled with gray moths, flittering every which way like a manic mayfly hatch. Thousands of them swirling and diving like little ghosts. The white aspen trees overhead bent and flung like palms in a hurricane. I thought a branch might break off, so I inchwormed my bag up against some downfall logs and tucked in.

Then I saw the fireflies. Everywhere. I bolted up, wrapped in my bag. There are no fireflies in the Gila. Burning embers marked the darkness with fermi lines and the moths were actually flakes of ash. Sparks from the fire had blown up the mountain. I won't say it was rational. First I thought, *I'll head back the way I came.* Then, *No, I need water down Spruce.* Then I thought, *Sometimes the world is more interesting than you like.* I thought that this could get dangerous and that I should take stock of what is possible and what is important. But I was just too tired for any sort of decision. I fell, again—this time, into a deep sleep.

This is the third way to fall, and it can happen in any time or place. It is the feeling of standing too close to the edge of a cliff, of roller-coaster rides, or driving too fast around a corner. It is the feeling of love. The fall is also the moment a needle touches an addict's arm, a loaded handgun is lifted, or a lie is told to a friend. And it is in the moment of contrition and forgiveness, in our loudest vows and curses. The one thing about falling is, as long as you can get up again things are still possible; it makes life interesting. The most interesting challenge we have is finding our place on this planet. If we want wilderness and wild places, it will not be an accident. It is going to take a lot of hard work, and most of the work will involve things that fall apart.

In the morning a breeze riffled the leaves overhead and it was all good—no ash or embers. So I got up, packed my things, and headed along the animal trails into Spruce Creek.

FLOW 100

"Yet one can always find solace in a living river. It is never still, never staid; hiding its prizes, providing glimpses, it holds a continual promise of things to come."

—M. H. "Dutch" Salmon
Gila Descending: A Southwestern Journey, 1986

LAURA PASKUS

WILD LOVE

ORN IN THE MOGOLLON MOUNTAINS IN SOUTHWESTERN
New Mexico, the Gila isn't a big river. Where it pours
from the Gila Wilderness, upstream of the tiny towns
of Cliff and Gila, it's the kind of stretch where little
kids splash on a hot summer day. A place to submerge
in the oh-so-clear water and kiss someone for the very first time.
To spot fish, stare up at the leaves, and daydream while listening
to the susurrus of water over stones.

But when storms set the Gila loose, it becomes a different
species, ripping up eighty-year-old cottonwoods and sycamores,
wedging them into twenty-foot-tall piles that reshape the floodplain. It rips out bridges and culverts, lays waste to anything in
its path.

That's in part because, in New Mexico, the Upper Gila isn't
dammed, though some irrigators do siphon off water for fields.
Meanwhile, downstream in Arizona, the hardworking river—
lashed behind dams and pent up in reservoirs—often dries up
long before meeting the Colorado River near Yuma.

But the Upper Gila remains one of the Southwest's few
streams not impacted in a major way by dams and diversions.
It's also a river most New Mexicans have likely never visited. It
takes some work to get there, and it traverses one of the least
populated parts of the state. But in the past decade, many have
come to love the river—perhaps because we almost lost it.

*

HOW THAT CAME TO PASS is a very long story.

I'll skip the US Supreme Court battles and details from the early to mid-twentieth century and jump to the 2000s, when Arizona was settling water rights with the Gila River Indian Community. To do so, the state needed federal money—and support from New Mexico senators Pete Domenici and Jeff Bingaman, alternating chairs of the powerful committee necessary to get the bill moving. So when Congress passed the Arizona Water Settlements Act of 2004, it included language allowing New Mexico to take advantage of some long-promised water rights on the Gila and its tributary, the San Francisco.

Those water rights came with a catch, though: this wasn't "wet water" in the river that New Mexico suddenly owned outright; people couldn't just divert it onto fields or through pipes. Instead, we needed a downstream partner willing to trade water for money. And the 2004 law finally set that up: under certain conditions, upstream New Mexicans could draw an annual fourteen thousand acre-feet of water out of the Gila, and then pay an exchange fee to the Gila River Indian Community, over in Arizona, which would use that money to buy Colorado River water. New Mexico could only use that water to meet future needs in four counties: Catron, Grant, Hidalgo, and Luna. The law allowed New Mexico lots of choices—it could use those water rights for a number of conservation and restoration projects—or it could build a diversion.

Complicated, right? I know. But there is one very important thing to remember: the law came with a pile of federal cash. The catch was, New Mexico would receive more money if it built a diversion—roughly $100 million versus $66 million.

Proponents coveted that fourteen thousand acre-feet of water—water that climate scientists and engineers showed was not even available from the system most years. Nonetheless, they set about concocting plans to pipe water over mountains to desert cities and to local farmers to grow crops like hay and alfalfa.

To be sure, this wasn't the first time someone floated big plans for the Gila. Decades earlier, the federal government had proposed three different dams here.

A few years ago, I sat in the National Archives in Washington, DC, and flipped through the letters people fired off in the late 1960s imploring the Senate Energy and Natural Resource Committee to keep its hands off the Gila and its wilderness. Men, women, and couples, faraway groups like the Texas Ornithological Society and the Methodist Church in Montana, all waxed poetic about protecting a river and a stretch of wilderness most of them had never seen.

In the 1980s there was another fight, this time over the proposed Connor Dam, on the Upper Gila. At that time, a Silver City writer and self-described "redneck environmentalist" named M. H. "Dutch" Salmon embarked on a two-hundred-mile trip down the Gila to draw attention to the travesty of that project. In a cheap Pullman canoe, Dutch brought along his dog and a black-and-white cat.

The trip started off in the pines and mountains and ended up in the Sonoran Desert. In New Mexico's upper stretches of the river, there's tremendous diversity. "It's probably the only place in the country you can see an elk and a coatimundi in the same day," Dutch told me a few years ago. "Or catch a wild trout and a flathead catfish out of the same pool." He taught his son to fly-fish in the Gila National Forest and spoke with pride of his son tracking down a mule deer buck by himself at age sixteen.

Thirty years later, Dutch had to fight for the Gila again.

IN 2003, ACTIVISTS AROUND SILVER City heard rumblings of Arizona's water settlement bill—and what New Mexico was hoping to get out of it.

In the past, plans for dams had bumped up against reality:

there was too little water available, and the dams cost money no one wanted to pay.

"That was always the big deal, no one actually had the money to construct the project, it was just too expensive," says Allyson Siwik, executive director of the conservation nonprofit Gila Resources Information Project (GRIP) and a fierce protector of the region. But this time, she and others heard there would be a federal subsidy for the diversion. And that changed everything.

The Upper Gila Watershed Alliance and the Center for Biological Diversity put renewed muscle behind the Gila Conservation Coalition, a loose group of volunteers assembled in 1984 to fight Connor Dam. They started applying for grants, recruiting volunteers, reaching out to technical experts, and pushing back against the rhetoric coming from state officials.

For years, the Gila Conservation Coalition, along with groups like Conservation Voters New Mexico, battled to have a say in how the money would be spent. They didn't just want to save the Gila from a dam; they also urged the state to resist pouring the entire subsidy into just one project. Money could be spread around to benefit lots of different communities, they argued, funding water conservation in cities and tightening up irrigation infrastructure on farms. These weren't just activists or environmentalists. The coalition included ranchers, farmers, even a mining company.

During the process, the state allowed cities, irrigators—any stakeholders in the region—to propose projects addressing water needs: everything from municipal water conservation programs to watershed restoration. But in 2014, the Interstate Stream Commission, appointed by Republican governor Susana Martinez, voted to approve a diversion estimated to cost over $1 billion. The structure was slated for just downstream of where the river flows out of the Gila Wilderness.

At the meeting in Albuquerque when commissioners made their plans official, Dutch was disappointed but not surprised. At the time, he told me, "We just got nine misguided individuals, and we'll hope to educate them better in the coming months and years ahead. I don't have any doubts about what will prevail in the end and keep our river as we've known it to be."

BY THIS STAGE IN THE FIGHT, Dutch was in his own battle with Parkinson's. But at every meeting I attended, he was there, reassuring people not to worry about the fate of the Gila River. At the time, I assumed he was giving me requisite sound bites for my coverage.

Now I understand better—he was just clear in his vision for the future of the river.

Dutch died in March 2019, so I can't ask him what he thinks about all this. But his wife, Cherie Salmon, says he got along with everyone—environmentalists, farmers, even diversion proponents—and didn't care if people disagreed with him.

"He didn't want to change minds," says Cherie. "He just felt he was on the right side of the diversion issue, and he was going to fight till he got it done."

And he didn't hold grudges. "People might get—I wouldn't say pissed at him—but it didn't bother him," she says. "He'd shake hands, say 'See you at the next meeting.'"

Recently, I listened to an interview I recorded with Dutch in 2014. I'd asked if he was reluctant to share some of his best fishing spots—like in the Upper Box, a riparian canyon with both pine trees and desert plants. He agreed that was typically hard to do: "Except in the case of the Gila," he said. "I'll give up a few secrets if it will gain us a few converts."

He waxed on about the bass and catfish, the black hawks and vermillion flycatchers. "It's just a lovely place to go—it's not a designated wilderness, just a de facto wilderness," he said. "It's a jewel about to be protected or smashed, depending on who wins."

I'll always remember leaving a meeting in July 2014, walking with Dutch out of the gymnasium of the Cliff High School. The humid air crackled with the electricity of a brewing storm. About one hundred people had been inside, listening to state officials talk about flow models and macroinvertebrates and economic analysis.

At the meeting that night, there had been a lot of questions and not many answers. But it was clear state officials wanted the diversion built. And they weren't going to listen to facts—not about climate change, not even about engineering flaws.

As Dutch and I stood at the edge of the darkening parking lot, he told me, "Don't worry. We'll get 'em."

AND SEE, HERE'S THE THING. They did get 'em.

After spending five years and nearly $20 million, diversion boosters never came up with a plan solid enough for study. And the weight of the project collapsed in upon itself. Which is peculiar, really. They had money and engineers. For eight solid years of the Martinez administration, they had political support. The US Bureau of Reclamation even held their hands through the planning process.

But with no plans in place, support from the federal government evaporated. The Trump administration's secretary of the interior denied their request for a time extension. And then, in 2020, acting on a campaign pledge, Democratic governor Michelle Lujan Grisham vetoed spending on the project. The new members of the Interstate Stream Commission voted to end work on studies for the diversion.

Now, with millions spent, the state needs to start all over again and decide what kinds of water projects to fund with the remainder of that federal subsidy.

Looking back, it's clear that diversion proponents had everything they needed to win a fight, particularly a fight over western water. They had the legal go-ahead. And they had access to power and money.

But they never seemed to have love in their hearts.

I'm not talking about the high-fructose corn syrup love of Valentine's Day. Or the love someone has for the preservation of their own lineage. I mean the wild love of first kisses and a future of possibilities. The love of sharing a planet with species who fill our skies and waters and soils. The love that comes with snipping loose our own desires and shoring up a better future for people and species we might never know.

For years as I reported on the Gila, I heard opponents of the diversion speak with tenderness and vulnerability.

One mother was inspired to protect the river by the activism and poetry of her teenaged daughter, who died in a plane crash over the Gila while surveying post-fire recovery as part of a school project. An engineer and former state official spoke of visiting the Gila as a kid and then surviving flood conditions on a rafting trip as an adult. One biologist described studying native fish, including rare spikedace and loach minnow, for more than thirty years—and what it felt like knowing they could blink out of existence in the coming years. Another marveled over the dynamism of the Gila's unique ecosystem.

Opponents of the diversion spoke of love, wonder, and their hopes for the future. And when they rallied support to protect the river—whether to stop the diversion or, later, to designate stretches of the Gila as Wild and Scenic—they invited people to love the Gila enough to protect it. As Siwik told me once, "I just feel it at the bottom of my heart, that we have to save this river."

Meanwhile, through both their victories and defeats, proponents of the diversion yelled about what they wanted, and about what others were denying them by asking about environmental impacts or questioning engineering flaws in their plans. In public meetings, they consistently misrepresented history, denied scientific facts, and told outrageous lies.

For years, Siwik says, proponents perpetuated a narrative of fear and scarcity. Fear that Arizona would take New Mexico's water. Fear that there wasn't enough to go around. At the same time, they didn't tell the truth about that water. Even if there were huge demands for water in the future, the Gila couldn't meet them. It's a tiny river, remember. That fourteen thousand acre-feet is on paper, not flowing down the riverbed.

Those hydrological realities, however, never seemed to matter. At a 2020 meeting, after the new governor's appointees to the Interstate Stream Commission voted to end funding, one member of the group planning the diversion called opponents an infection that was spreading like a cancer. Siwik still feels stung by those words from someone within her own community.

But it's clear that the ugliness of their need, of their words, of their hate was never a match for love.

Dutch must have known that when he told me years ago not to worry. I think the rain clouds above us that night sparked and spit not as a warning but a promise. And I know that when the river floods, it does so not in vengeance, to knock out culverts and bridges and wreak havoc on fields. Rather, its wild power lies with loving the floodplain enough to change its course for the future.

THE SPRINGS

WHEN I WAS GROWING UP, MY FATHER KEPT A photo on his desk of a place deep in the Gila Wilderness. The picture showed him at a younger age, maybe in his twenties, soaking in a small mountain pool with a friend. They looked like they were in the prime of life, in on the secret of mother nature. He told me it was Jordan Hot Springs, and I thought to myself, *That must be what it's all about.*

I'd often call that picture to mind in times of stress or worry. After college, I lived in New York, and I saw Jordan Hot Springs one hot summer morning on my way to work as a proofreader at a publishing company in the Bronx. My commute involved two trains and forty-five minutes in each direction. Crammed into the 4 Train without air conditioning, sweating and stressed about life and work, pressed up against a hundred other people also stressed about life and work, that picture of my dad and the Gila and the great outdoors opened up a vista in my mind and put a smile on my face. I thought about it all day. After I clocked out, I walked into my supervisor's office and gave her my two weeks' notice. "I'm moving back to Texas," I said.

I started backpacking with my dad in southern New Mexico when I was old enough to walk and continued through my school years. Sometimes we'd go up with my younger sisters, sometimes with family friends, but mostly it was the two of us and the family dog, Woody.

We'd leave El Paso after school on Friday and head into one

of the great public lands nearby—the Lincoln National Forest, the Aldo Leopold Wilderness, or the Gila Wilderness—where we'd make the trailhead before evening and hike in a few miles to a campsite. Our first night's meal was always Kraft macaroni and cheese and Knorr's oxtail soup.

During the day we'd throw the frisbee at the campsite (over the fire, in between trees, off the side of the tent), read, hike to a nearby peak or fire lookout, or just nap with the wind blowing by and birds talking to each other. Pre-dinner snack was usually a tin of sardines in mustard sauce or smoked oysters on Triscuits.

My dad died twenty years ago, hit by a car while riding his bike outside El Paso. But those times together in the Gila are fixed in my memory. He never talked to me on those trips about conservation or the importance of protecting public lands. But I'm not sure if that was necessary for him to get the point across.

I was six years old, crossing a stream with my dad on one of the first overnight backpacks that I can remember. He stopped, balanced on the rocks midstream, unhooked his tin cup from his pack, dipped it into the water, and drank it down. I followed his lead and did the same. I now know that you're not supposed to drink straight from a water source in the outdoors without filtering it. But, at least in my memory, I have never in my life drunk water so good and so refreshing. The cold mineral taste, the tin cup on my teeth and lips, the immediacy of the limitless reward—you just dip your cup when you're thirsty!

Over the years we explored the massive Gila as well as the adjoining Aldo Leopold Wilderness from what seemed like all over. Sometimes we'd hike in from the visitors' center, and on the return trip home grab an ice cream at Doc Campbell's store. Other trips we'd start near Hillsboro and Emory Pass Vista. Sometimes we'd drive close to the Arizona border and come in from the western edge of the Gila, which recalls a memory of playing Asteroids in a bar in Glenwood in the early 1980s while my dad and a friend drank a beer after we'd hiked the Catwalk

Trail (I was completely fascinated by the trail's metal walkway, attached to the canyon wall, and the narrow swinging bridges, mining relics rebuilt by the Civilian Conservation Corps).

But no matter how many trips we took, how many different trailheads we started from, we never got close to seeing all of it.

AFTER MOVING BACK TO TEXAS from New York in my early twenties, I started to walk into the Gila by myself or invite friends to join me, usually to familiar places that I'd been to with my dad.

These special places and everything I associate with the Gila—the river crossings and welcome pools of water, the animals I've met (a herd of javelina; a lone bear cub with her mother close by, I'm sure; the lizards and rodents; even the bugs), the time with my dad, the friends I've taken in with me, the adventures with my wife, Amy (I proposed to her in the Gila), and our kids, the nights alone I spent looking up at the sky—are all memories I return to when the world of cities and politics isn't making sense.

I also think about the air locks through which I passed every time I came out of the Gila, those places in between that are necessary to fully process the journey before seeing family and familiar places back home—and essential to satisfying the ravenous hunger built up on the trail. There's nothing quite like the taste of a gloriously messy green chile cheeseburger and a cold beer at the Barbershop Café in Hillsboro after you've just walked out of the wilderness. I remember many an ice cream with my dad at Doc Campbell's, near the Gila Visitors' Center; and the time I ate the hottest plate of enchiladas in Deming with college friends I'd just introduced to the Gila, trying to tough the food down so as not to let on that it was burning my insides.

Those immediate post-Gila experiences are richer, the food better—so good I can remember it years later—for the nights slept under the open sky, the miles walked through the forest trails, and the blisters and scrapes earned along the way.

No backpack in the Gila was ever easy, and some trips truly tested me. But somehow, what makes the Gila tough and unforgiving is also what makes it great.

One January many years ago, I backpacked into the Black Range with Dave, a good friend from Philadelphia, and my two dogs. We hiked in from Emory Pass Vista and walked a few miles along a ridgeline through steady falling snow. The little pond at nine thousand feet where we set up camp was completely covered in snow and ice, peaceful and beautiful on that still evening. We made dinner, drank a little whiskey, and, after the fire died down, looked up at the clear sky that was looking back down on us, pointing out the constellations we knew, or thought we knew.

We awoke to heavy snowfall. After packing up, we started our walk through a snowpack that at times was above our knees, intent upon reaching Holden Prong saddle before it got too late. But before we made it half a mile, the snowfall turned to a cold rain.

We lost the trail and just trudged through the mix of ice, snow, and mud until we finally made the saddle, exhausted, blown out, done. We made camp and tried to fry a steak in our tent, but we were both so wet and cold and exhausted and maybe a little worried, as the rain turned back to snow and the wind howled without break, that we couldn't eat. So I gave the steak to the also very wet and cold and worried dogs, curled up and shivering at our feet.

When we woke the next day, everything was ice. The wind was whipping and whistling past the frozen tent, rattling the aspens just below us in Gallinas Canyon. Why had we kept pushing deeper into the wilderness when the weather was so bad? If it kept snowing like this, how were we going to get out? I kept waiting for the weather to break, for the sun to come out, for the wind to at least stop blowing. But it only got worse. The roar of the wind grew louder, the sky darker. It looked hopeless. We willed ourselves out of the tent and tried to pack up.

I can't remember ever being that cold. I couldn't get my hands to work; they were too numb and painful, down to the bone, to work the zipper on my jacket or break down the tent or stuff my sleeping bag down into the bottom of my pack. Finally, after rubbing them together raw and almost warm—working a little, warming a little, cursing and jumping around to get my blood flowing—I was able to get packed up enough to commence our long freezing miserable march to the trailhead. I mostly kept my head down to save my face from the sting of the wind, but when I'd look up to get my bearings, the landscape was still stunning. Big, majestic Douglas firs, standing like mighty bulwarks against the storm, gave way to juniper and piñon as we approached the ridgeline. There, the vista opened up so that we could see down and out along Railroad Canyon, covered in snow, trees whipping back and forth, and the wind blowing like a train right up that canyon to the saddle we'd slept on the night before. When we finally came out at the Emory Pass trailhead, there was another group of backpackers from El Paso making their way in. We warned them about the conditions, but they had a case of beer on their backs, big goofy smiles on their faces, and no intention of stopping before they started. "Good luck," we said.

The Blake's Lotaburger on the way home never tasted so good.

I'VE TAKEN MY DAUGHTER and two boys to the Gila a dozen or so times, not as much as I'd like, and not as often as my dad took me. There's usually some small protest from them, and I've always got enough work that it's easy to agree to postpone the trip for another time. But even if we only go once or twice a year, it's always a powerful experience.

In some ways, the place seems just as it did when I went for the first time forty-five years ago. In other ways, it's different. The trails have degraded enough in some places that they functionally don't exist, forcing us to use the GPS on my phone to stay on track. There's also a lot more fire damage than I remember from my time as a kid.

But we usually have the trails to ourselves, and the experience is always worthwhile—in other words, whatever complaining was going on, whatever work I have waiting for me back home, I can hear the fascination in my kids' voices as we talk about what we just experienced on the drive out. We've heard mountain lions calling to each other at night, seen the ground carpeted in new flowers in the spring, played in creeks and rivers, told stories by the fire, slept under moonless skies. We briefly give ourselves over to this ancient land on these trips, and I hope in doing so we are creating memories for our kids as powerful as my dad did for me.

During the summer of 2020, my wife organized a road trip through Colorado, trying to make the best of our isolation in the pandemic by getting the five of us outside and away from screens and devices. We hiked a fourteener, swam and fished in Twin Lakes, below Mount Elbert, and walked under waterfalls and alongside glacial pools outside Silverton.

It was all beautiful, sometimes staggeringly so. But I couldn't help but notice how easy most of it felt. Not physically—some of those hikes are tough. But the experience of being outside in Colorado is relatively convenient for the visitor. Signage is plentiful, parking always available, the trails manicured to a degree unfamiliar to those of us in West Texas or southern New Mexico.

The other thing that struck me was just how many people there were out there. It was packed. Everywhere. At some points on our climb from Mineral Creek to Ice Lake, near Silverton, we found ourselves backed up in traffic jams twenty to thirty people deep. Too many people, not enough trail. At one tight bend coming down, we stepped off to allow a family of four and their rented alpacas to pass on their way to one of the few remaining campsites.

It was a lot different from the Gila, where, though it's a little rougher and more out of the way, you might not meet another person no matter how many miles you hike in a day. You have the expanse and the magic of this natural heritage to yourself. The Gila is less curated, wilder and more raw—and, for me, it's heaven on earth.

I FINALLY DID FIND JORDAN Hot Springs. Three years before my dad died, when I first started going into the Gila on my own, I asked him for directions.

"You'll go to Deming," he said, "and then make the turn towards City of Rocks. Go past Mimbres, up near the visitors' center, and then look for the trailhead at TJ Corral."

From there he described a journey of long climbs and steep descents before we'd pass through a tight canyon that would lead to one of the forks of the Gila River. Then there'd be a series of river crossings, "seventeen or eighteen," before we'd come upon the spring-fed hot tub.

"You can't miss it," he promised.

In fact, I did miss it on that first attempt. Against his advice, I tried to walk down from the Meadows, a beautiful spot a few miles upstream from Jordan, certain that I could find the springs if I just kept crossing the Middle Fork enough times. However, on the next trip a friend and I followed my father's prescribed path, up through Little Bear Canyon, where the walls reach up to form a towering cathedral of rock, reminding me of Gaudí's rambling, majestic basilica in Barcelona.

Sure enough, on the eighteenth crossing we came upon the legendary pool from my dad's picture—the water held in by a small dam of rocks and earth, steam rising to meet the overhanging branches of the trees that surround it. Below the surface, it was as clear and clean as you could want. A holy place.

PRIYANKA KUMAR

JADE MOTHER

N THE SUMMER YOU LOOK FOR A RIVER THE WAY YOU LOOK FOR a cool breeze. In the winter you gravitate toward water because it's the animating force of a desert, and you find yourself meandering with her, inhaling her music, riveted by the birds that cleave to her. Back home, the river you live with is arrow straight—she has been harnessed by humans for so long, she has forgotten how to meander. In the Gila National Forest, however, the river leads you. If you've forgotten how to meander, the jade-green river will teach you. You don't have to go anywhere to look for birds—they simply weave around her bank. Thoreau said something like this once, that the best way to see birds is to sit down someplace and let the birds come to you.

Last winter I started with a creek and worked my way up to the river. I hadn't been to the Gila in some time, and after a six-hour drive, on my first evening back, I hiked down to Bear Creek as the sun was dipping. No sooner did I begin hiking than a motley flock of birds fled to two mature junipers. A surprising flash of red, on inspection, proved to be a northern cardinal, *Cardinalis cardinalis*, pomegranate-colored with a striking black face mask; through the foliage, the male's dark brown eyes watched me somberly. Among the others was a luminous white-crowned sparrow, *Zonotrichia leucophrys*. To my left, the Pinos Altos Mountains, where the creek originates, were lit up with alpenglow. This pink-and-tan range dominates the southern end of the Gila Wilderness, the mountains' distinctive sedimentary layers harking back to their deep-sea origins. Now they exhaled soft gilded pinks and grays, so radiant they seemed to glow from within.

Down I went, skirting a honey mesquite as its bold white thorns snagged my jeans. I flushed a handful of white-winged doves, *Zenaida asiatica*. White-winged doves are more slender, their curves more elegant, than the mourning doves I see in my backyard. With the poise and vanity of flamenco dancers, wearing flashy blue orbital rings around their orange irises, they fluttered and chattered before settling in for the night.

I was losing my battle with light as I approached Bear Creek. The creek is a mere cub who, twenty miles from where it begins, joins the mother bear that is the 640-mile Gila River. The creek murmured and soothed as the sun slipped beyond the horizon, reflecting ten thousand beams of light. To my right, coral pink rippled into the blue-gray sky. As I lingered, a lone ruby-crowned kinglet, *Regulus calendula,* hopped in a bare tree, solitary but perhaps content, like me, to be breathing beauty.

IN THIS SOUTHWESTERN SECTION of the Gila National Forest, the prickly pear cacti are plate-sized and colored like the inside of an avocado. Recalling those cacti, the river begins her life forked, the headwaters of her three prongs—East, West, and Middle— flowing through the nine hundred square miles we call the Gila Wilderness. With a mother's love, she brings together disparate biomes—the Chihuahuan and the Sonoran Deserts and subalpine fir forests, to name just three.

A watershed is an integral part of a wilderness area; Aldo Leopold believed this too. When he was a Forest Service employee, the service's "highest use" philosophy translated into harvesting more lumber. But in 1919, Leopold would meet a more like-minded colleague after hearing about young Arthur Carhart's work in Colorado. When tasked with surveying how many lots the Forest Service should lease for the construction of summer cottages along Trappers Lake, in the state's Flat Tops range, Carhart had advocated for a revolutionary number—zero. He successfully argued that the lake's beautiful shoreline should be protected instead for generations to come.

Leopold heard about Carhart's report in December 1919, at a Forest Service meeting in Salt Lake City, and, on his way back to Albuquerque, he stopped by Carhart's district office. In a daylong meeting that would produce America's first "wilderness memo," the two men agreed that the onslaught on public lands was already very aggressive—national parks were being criss-crossed with roads and facilities to make them more accessible to visitors, and national forests were being cut up with roads to make them more accessible to lumber companies. Leopold believed that, before it was too late, some wild areas ought to be spared the "marring features of man-made constructions." A little later, he circulated among his Albuquerque colleagues his long-simmering plan for a wilderness area in the Gila National Forest, and he put forward a formal proposal in October 1922.

At a time when the term "wilderness" wasn't in the parlance of the Forest Service, Leopold's plan met with some quiet sympathy, but also with opposition among lumber enthusiasts and within the Service itself. Leopold, however, foresaw that the Gila area—scarcely of any agricultural use—offered high recreational value to the kind of "sportsman" who, like himself, favored backpacking for a couple of weeks without encountering such thing as a road. Years later, on one trip with his sons along the Gila River in November 1927, Leopold made regular entries in his journal—but his mind was on shooting deer, not so much on the beauty of the river that he had been surprisingly effective in protecting.

I HIKED THE NEXT DAY through a riparian area downstream from Pancho Canyon, a jewel in the desert; in the southwestern

United States, only 2 percent of our landscape remains riparian. In Latin, *ripa* means riverbank, and riparian habitat crucially links terrestrial and aquatic habitats.

The river was straighter here, not meandering as by the Old Iron Bridge along old US 180, where I had begun my morning hike. There was an air of desolation in that stretch, and someone's coyote-like dog tailed me too closely. I brightened where the water picked up speed around an S-shaped curve, and paused to listen to a song sparrow, *Melospiza melodia*, warbling among a host of white-crowned sparrows. The wintering song sparrow is a riparian obligate, a species that biologists define as almost exclusively occupying aquatic habitats. With the air of a Pavarotti, it sang full throttle to the river as she curved, glittering, over a bed of stones.

Near Pancho Canyon, I found a steady log to eat lunch where the river seemed a denser green, more subject to inertia. The cottonwoods towered, the habitat was more continuous here, and the birds paid a nod to this fact, for a panoply of stunners wafted by. I had glimpsed a belted kingfisher, *Megaceryle alcyon*, here before, and I trusted that if I sat down by the river the kingfisher would come to me. It did. The bird, with a blue-green head and an imperial white stripe running around its neck, flew along the river, dead center, until it reached a bare tree growing toward the water, the bough curving into the river as though bowing to her. The kingfisher alighted on the apex of this curve, but I only managed a quick, clear look through binoculars before the bird rose and resumed its flight upriver; royalty grants only a fleeting gaze.

Moving away from the river, in the dead of winter, there is little sign of animal life. And you give up looking. But then a desert bird flashes by, bringing delight in its wake—the incongruous red of a male cardinal flying over the dirt path, a Gambel's quail, *Callipepla gambelii*, skittering by on the ground. A greater roadrunner, *Geococcyx californianus*, dares to show itself—a flaneur on its daily stroll, unperturbed by gawking eyes. Birds like the quail and the roadrunner tune me into the hidden rhythms, into the pulse, of the desert land.

THE NEXT MORNING, I GAZED across the valley bottom at the long range of mud-colored Big Burro Mountains, clusters of whole-wheat dough balls set to rise. I couldn't help but marvel at the coincidence of spotting two burros in someone's shed, their gray-brown backs smooth, also rising and falling like freshly made loaves of bread.

As the morning wore on, a little canyon wren, *Catherpes mexicanus*, explored an embankment along the river, poking its distinctive white face into one hole in the mud or another until it found just the thing—a cavern with a semicircular arch and a sound ceiling. Slipping into this wondrous natural structure, the wren vanished from sight, away from the heating shafts of the noonday sun. The river gurgled approvingly, speaking in a tongue that we no longer know, but which the canyon wren still comprehends. There were others who intuited the river's mean-ing. When Indigenous peoples lived unmolested on this land, they were superb watchers of animal movements. I imagine that they saw wrens and other animals make use of natural caverns, sometimes as nesting holes. The day before, I had climbed up into the Gila Cliff Dwellings, a village-in-a-cavern, wedged into a cliff face, where some inhabitants of the Mogollon had lived. As I stood breathing in the fine white dust, I saw in my mind's eye the green torrents that had led almost up to this cliff. The Mogollon cavern had an arch eerily similar to the wren's cavern, albeit with spectacular rooms carpentered inside that are still standing after more than seven hundred years.

Sometimes you come upon the river's old routes, all silt and stone, and you marvel that the jade river once flew and sang past here. An Arizona state historian tells us that the name of the

Gila River in Spanish means roughly "a steady going to or coming from someplace." The Gila is one of the longest rivers in the West, but she dries up, due to human diversions, before reaching the Colorado River. These diversions sap her flow, which leads to a decline in woody native riparian plants and increased tree mortality, as a Nature Conservancy report recently noted, which in turn renders the habitat less suitable for nesting birds.

I hiked farther up where the trail diverged from the river. Hearing some rustling among a bed of dried cottonwood leaves, I paused, expecting to see a spotted towhee scratching among the leaves. But it was a larger animal. Presently, the snow-white face of a skunk and then its black-and-white body, so lavishly attired by nature, showed itself. The animal moved with a solemn, deliberate air. I saw it in profile, just a few feet away, before it turned and shuffled across a dry bed to the river for a long midday draught.

The river suckles the canyon wren and the towhee and the skunk. During my time in the Gila, she was mother to me too, offering her bank, her lap—a place to return to and listen to the music of birds.

A MOTHER HAS HER DANGERS: the Gila River is prone to flash-floods, and mountain lions roam through her floodplains. On another afternoon, my husband, Michael, and I saw urgent warning signs, cautioning us about mountain lion sightings. The signs weren't the usual mountain lion signs we've seen over the years, white, with a line drawing of a mountain lion; they were newer, red signs, larger so you wouldn't miss them, and with specific instructions, such as, do not run when you see a mountain lion. They asked that we "pick up small children"; we had both of ours with us.

We found another trail, without the signs but with similar habitat—tall grass, thorny mesquite, yucca. I tailed my younger one as though I were her shadow, noting how small she is. The old floodplain that lay before us, covered thickly with chamisa, was wide open and without fences: it looked to be prime lion territory.

We hiked up to a clearing and picnicked. Michael stood on guard; he never once sat down. We were surrounded by a golden, grassy silence. The chamisa swayed in the slight wind. Of course, a mountain lion is also tawny colored and would be camouflaged in this field. The molten core of the field permeated me. I dissolved into the yellow rays of the sun. *It* was drifting somewhere, invisible in the grass, its lithe muscular body twitching at the slightest sound; I stopped imagining, I didn't want to summon the animal. But there was no getting away from the yellow thought of the lion. There was something that linked us. The very remoteness that had attracted me to this area is also what attracts the mountain lion. The sandwich bread felt dry in my throat. I munched some celery and stood up abruptly, startled.

When the question came up of whether we should go on hiking up to the rusty coyote willow and beyond, to the river in the distance, a mother's fear flashed through my heart and we decided to turn around. Once we got back to the trailhead, our children had many questions about mountain lions, and, in calming their anxieties, we grew calmer, too.

THE GILA WOODPECKER, *MELANERPES UROPYGIALIS*, isn't a common bird in its namesake forest. But I found three at once on adjoining Nature Conservancy land. One, its head the color of a kiwi fruit, let out a series of high-pitched mews as it flew from one cottonwood to the next, all three woodpeckers playing a game of musical chairs on the bare trees. In an adjacent field, a pair of pearl-gray sandhill cranes let out throaty, gurgling calls, calling out to another pair, back and forth, while six other cranes glided by, as though there can't be too much beauty in a singular moment. In the heart of the desert, you are moved by such abundance.

The late afternoon light was incandescent; it had something of the quality of the blazing logs I would stare into later that night. The day's last light pooled in my children's faces as they raced alongside the field the cranes had claimed as their own. Like the woodpecker and the cranes, the Gila River is free to come and go as she pleases, to meander here, to straighten there, to rush on in ten thousand rivulets elsewhere. Because of the vision of certain people who came before us—Aldo Leopold is one—the Upper Gila hasn't been straightened, harnessed, or dammed in any major way; hasn't been damned to wear a concrete straitjacket.

In June 1924, days after Leopold left the region to work for a Forest Products Lab in Wisconsin, his former supervisor in Albuquerque, Frank Pooler, approved his cherished Recreation Plan by administrative fiat. It designated 755,000 acres of the Gila Forest as a wilderness area—the first such action taken anywhere in the world. At the time there was no legal framework guaranteeing that the land would remain protected. That would have to wait another forty years, for the passage of the Wilderness Act in 1964.

Today the river's freedom is in our hands. Will its wild spirit go on blazing? Will it go on being an amphitheater to celestial birdsong? It would be unimaginable if the belted kingfisher ceased to fly over bare branches, or if the river were barred from flowing where she pleased. It's in her freedom that the Gila River is wild, and it's her wildness that makes her an anomalous, mythic river. Freedom and wildness are braided together, inseparable—they make each other whole. The river's first set of children—the birds and the animals, the kingfisher and the mountain lion—need this wholeness even more than we do.

LEEANNA T. TORRES

GOYAHKLA

SOMEWHERE NEAR THE TOP OF RAW MEAT CANYON, I SIT
waiting for the time to pass. The treatment is almost
complete. The bucket slowly leaking toxic fluid into
the middle of the stream is almost empty. This mountain canyon of the West Fork of the Gila River is made
of trees and rock and water, and I sit here in the heart of the
wilderness, wishing I had another sandwich, wishing it wasn't
raining.

Crouched under a tree, I hold the hood of my jacket steady
over my head and face. The pines above me aren't enough to
keep the rain off; water falls right past their needles. The rain
seems to leak right through the Gore-Tex, its waterproofness
long ago worn away on field trips like this.

Our trip began with a one-night stay at the Heart Bar. Owned
by the New Mexico Department of Game and Fish, the small
two-bedroom cabin serves as a base camp for the scientific community. It's a small, humble house full of spiderwebs and whiskey. There were seven of us set to pack in; we looked more like
renegades than scientists, already dusty, already drinking on a
Tuesday night before eight days of solid work in the Wilderness.

There is no magic about our work. We kill non-native fish in
order to reestablish native Gila trout, one of the original species
listed under the Endangered Species Act in 1973. The US Fish
and Wildlife Service is responsible for these restoration efforts,
and I work for the agency. I am a biologist working on saving a
fish. But to save one fish, we have to kill others.

We treat the streams with antimycin, a chemical piscicide used in fisheries management. It's all applied science, here in these mountains. The basis for this trip, and all the work, is science, strictly science, and yet since we left the Heart Bar, I have been distanced from this thing called *science*. Instead, I am distracted by a spirit.

Geronimo is said to have been born in these mountains, near the source of the Gila River, around 1823. He was given the name Goyahkla, "the one who yawns"—the appellation Geronimo would only come years later, bestowed by Mexican forces during their many conflicts with the Apache people. I think of him fishing in this same stream as a young man, so much struggle and battle and death still ahead of him. History tells us that Mexican soldiers murdered his mother and wife, his three young children.

Our team had set out into the Gila Wilderness on horseback, with pack mules trailing behind. I'd done this seven-hour ride before, but still I took in all the scenery like a tourist. Pines and bluffs, blue sky and heated sun—riding into the Gila is always like seeing things for the first time. We passed through the large section of piñon and juniper burned in a 1996 fire. We passed by cliff dwellings not sketched on any map, and through the valley of McKenna Park, with small yellow flowers blooming between the grasses. Throughout the ride, I thought of only one thing: Goyahkla's ghost, lurking somewhere near, as close as all my insecurities and fears.

NOTHING DRIES HERE IN THE GILA—not pants, not socks, not shirts. The drenching afternoon storms ruin the morning sun's efforts. These monsoon rains are as unpredictable as my brother's moods—sometimes it pours throughout these mountains; other times the rain chooses only one single canyon. But today it's coming down hard, and the antimycin seems to be taking longer than usual to do its work.

The upper Gila River is the last of its kind in the Southwest. No large dams impede its natural flow. For much of the twentieth century, New Mexico's last free-flowing river has been under threat of certain change from dam and diversion projects. And yet it is not the science, not the geology, not the policy, that grounds me here. It's this sense of something stronger, something more subtle and yet hauntingly unmistakable.

I have felt Goyahkla's spirit: sharp, colored cream and yellow, brown sugar and juniper dust. It blows through, unlike a wind and more like a sound that is yellow and red and green. I feel it strong now, here in this canyon, as the rain seems to slow, and a wide patch of sunlight opens out on the surface of the stream.

On the West Fork, we often work in teams, but sometimes we're sent out alone for the day. We might measure out five-hundred-meter sections of stream with hammered-in rebar or write down information to evaluate and track habitat. Today we are setting out buckets equipped with copper valves to release the antimycin. Stephanie and Cody are on the White Creek tributary, while Johnny is waiting for me somewhere far below, in charge of his own orange buckets and yellow field notebook. Everyone has a job to do.

Many mainstream encyclopedias try to teach us about Geronimo. One calls him an Apache warrior, another an Apache leader. Trained as a medicine man, he first learned the secrets of healing and ceremony before acquiring his reputation as a fierce fighter who led raids on troops and settlers. The thin encyclopedias don't tell the whole history. They contain only small, splintered paragraphs containing what we are supposed to believe as facts, as truth.

My time in the Gila has taught me that there is nothing romantic about restoration. Applied science here is as strict as stone. The work makes me tired. My ankles are sore from trekking in cobble and fast-moving water all day. My feet hurt, my clothes are wet, and I'm tired. And for what? A fish? I put my hands in the water, feel the cold, and keep them there until they go numb. It's August, but the stream water is cold. Only trout like it this cold. All this work and ache for a fish species that may not even make it. I listen to the water for something beyond all of this.

What I hear is the sound of Goyahkla, moving in and out of the sound of water. This water, sweeping over stone, with no time for anything sedentary, no time for anything other than movement. I feel the sound of Goyahkla, as wet as rain, as serious as thunder. And yet I wonder if any of the others hear it?

Johnny snores. Vern drinks too much. Stephanie places snuff in the space of her lower lip. Art tells us how he told off one of the regional deputy directors—loud, angry, unapologetic. Dave cooks up chili so spicy it's painful to eat. And Jim teases me about wearing a pink shirt out here in the first great wilderness of the United States, where men become men. These are my coworkers. Their concern is science and data; their concern is the whiskey. I wonder why I am here, a young Chicana biologist thinking about an Apache man who lived and died long before I came into existence. Why does this restoration project seem so far from important?

THE GILA WILDERNESS IS AS LARGE and expansive as an ocean. It is over five hundred thousand acres of undisturbed forest land, most of it unaccustomed to the blunt interruptions of human society. No stores, no streetlights, no roads, no eighteen-wheelers. There is only the rawness of the earth, in all its beauty and terror. The only sounds are the birds, the water, the shuffling wildlife, your own fearful heartbeat when you realize just how far you are from civilization.

Like so many things in our spectacular, amazing, privileged American life, I take "wilderness" for granted. I take the national parks, the federal forest system, the designated wilderness areas, all for granted. Of course, there was great controversy, battle, struggles for their creation, but they exist now, and they are a part of our heritage. Bold, brave, even arrogant men had the insight to create these areas for *us*, the American public. But was it *taken* or was it *preserved*? Was it *stolen* or was it *designated*? Geronimo and his Chiricahua Apache comrades finally surrendered to US troops in 1886. Goyahkla was forced to live out his days at Fort Sill, Oklahoma, where he was considered a tourist attraction.

Wilderness is not a romantic notion. It's not just a concept. It's a truth here in the lands of New Mexico. Yet few American citizens—even New Mexico residents themselves—will experience this wilderness for what it really is. I get to be here only because my work has brought me here. I am fortunate. I am blessed. But I am also worn-torn and ugly-tired from this work, this profession I've chosen, this job that pays the bills.

Walking in the stream with felt-bottomed boots, I manage to fall at least a dozen times a day. Vern turns and asks if I'm okay. Then he laughs when he sees how clumsy I look, sitting in the water. Stephanie lends me some muscle balm at the end of each day. And each day, even after all the work is done, even after the science and restoration and management is complete, we've still got an hour or more of walking back downstream to camp, and horses to feed, and a fire to make. Rest is a concept without color here in the Gila.

Conversations in the wilderness kitchen sound like any others among coworkers. We talk about books we've read, or the political goings-on at the various field offices. We tell stories. We tell jokes. We tell lies. Our conversations are ordinary. Or are they? Around the fire, we speak of our failures, but never of our desperations or our secrets or our private ceremonies of redemption. Around the fire, I don't tell Vern or Johnny or Stephanie or Jim about who or what I really am.

I am a contradiction, a Chicana biologist, one who claims to love the land yet is here killing fish. I am a mixed breed who can claim no one heritage or culture. Wanting to be a success, a lady, someone who is worth something, and yet I sneak swigs of hard whiskey on nights when no one is watching. I am a wilderness even to myself.

THE ANTIMYCIN TREATMENT IS ALMOST complete. I check my watch. The rain stops and I listen to my own breath, wait for the song of the birds to return. Then suddenly a fluttering of color wakes my senses, and hundreds of lavender butterflies appear. Some fly close to the surface, past the orange bucket still dripping piscicide, and up the canyon wall and into a sky I cannot see. Others flutter around the pines and willow and oak. Everywhere there are butterflies, and I can't explain where they've come from or why they're here.

I watch them for a very long time. The butterflies are not watching me; they are not trying to tell me anything; they just are, and even in my technically trained, university-educated mind, I do not search for a reason. I only know that this mountain wants me; it wants all of me. And just as the Gila gathers all storms into itself, it will also gather me.

New Mexico, the great Southwest, the land of my birth, is a cauldron of half-breeds, mixed blood—this is a historical fact. There are and have been Comancheros—half-breeds. There are and have been mestizos—mixed Spanish and Indian blood.

This is my history: mixed blood, impure. And here we are in the Gila, trying to save the "pure" strain of trout by killing off the mixed, the unwanted, the impure.

So, what is *my* Native ancestry? Where is the truth of myself? Somewhere in this wilderness? At the bottom of a bottle? It lies deep, as close as my own mother. They say I look like my father, but my blood is from my mother, and she gives me a history similar to that of Geronimo. I feel my blood shift. It stirs deep in the insides of my arms, a strain that makes my hands tired and my eyes fall.

It is then that the wilderness becomes my own. I'm five days covered in dirt and horse and mountain and sun and rain and shadow and absolute weariness. The Gila keeps me as honest as a prayer.

I give myself up completely. In essence, maybe I *am* a prayer. This is my lowest self, but this is also my best self, because I'm reduced to nothing. For once in my life, I am a prayer strong enough to offer up to the Spirit.

The Gila is always larger than any one part of myself. The Gila is larger than life. And the spirit of Geronimo—Goyahkla— tugs at every part of my soul. He was here with me on the ride in, and he is here with me now, in this canyon, and part of me is afraid.

Goyahkla is more than man, more than Apache, more than legend, more than a historic figure pictured between black and white and commentary. He haunts the long hard silences of this Gila Wilderness. He is the solidness of stone that trips your feet. He is the ache you feel in your joints after a day of work. He is that silence that stops you between the trees. Goyahkla is that sense of unsteadiness you feel when you realize just how large this expanse really is, and just how absolutely and utterly small you are.

Lightning. Rain. Wilderness. Science. Pine. Juniper. Water. Pain. These are the words, the simple words of this journey. And yet they are not enough. They are not enough.

I see him now, moving in the pattern of butterflies. I am not really a scientist. I am not really anyone at all. The fish in the stream are dead, by my hand, by the hand of science. All I can do is offer a prayer. A Tohono O'odham rain song, a song as old as the memory of time. I say it, I sing it, I sketch it into the lines of this mountain with an ache in my heart.

HOWL 100

Remember the earth whose skin you are:

red earth, black earth, yellow earth, white

earth

brown earth, we are earth.

Remember the plants, trees, animal life who

all have their

tribes, their families, their histories, too. Talk

to them,

listen to them. They are alive poems.

—Joy Harjo
From "Remember"

MARTIN HEINRICH

STILL BURNING BRIGHT

O N MY FIRST TRIP INTO THE GILA, I WENT SEARCHING for wolves. It was 1996, and I'd just taken an Ameri-Corps position with the US Fish and Wildlife Service, with the group working on Mexican wolf recovery. Mexican wolves are the most endangered and genetically unique subspecies of the North American gray wolf. They had been extirpated from the Gila and the rest of the Southwest by the mid-1900s and had only survived thanks to a small number of wolves captured from the wild in Mexico in the 1970s. By 1996, plans to restore the lobo to its home range were moving forward. My AmeriCorps colleagues and I were tasked with gathering data to dispel the rumors—persistent among some ranchers and other opponents of wolf reintroduction—that Mexican wolves still populated the mountains, mesas, and forests of the Southwest.

How does one do that exactly? I was about to find out. Two of us at a time would load a well-worn Fish and Wildlife truck with camping gear and head out into the backcountry for ten days at a time, surveying huge swaths of New Mexico and Arizona. Typically, we'd hike or drive a route, stopping every mile to howl into the darkness, once in each cardinal direction. Then we would record the responses.

A proper wolf howl starts high, drops an octave, and ends with a mournful tremolo. Despite our best efforts, no wolves ever responded. We did, however, record a plethora of coyote calls and—surprisingly—an amazing array of owl hoots, ranging from Mexican spotted owls to tiny elf owls. One Mexican spotted owl responded to my howl by flying up to the top of a dead tree fifteen feet away and inspecting me sharply, as if to say, "You don't look like a wolf."

In the process, we created a data set that was used to successfully defend the recovery project in court when it was challenged as unnecessary. As a result, by 2020, 186 endangered lobos called New Mexico and Arizona home, 114 of those in the greater Gila region.

THE GILA WAS ALSO MY first exposure to such a huge and dynamic landscape. I will never forget sitting at the edge of Cooney Prairie, north of the rugged Gila Wilderness, and watching wildlife mingle like wildebeest and impala on the African savanna. Elk, mule deer, and pronghorn antelope came and went as I watched through binoculars from under a tree at the edge of the massive grassy park. Wildlife I had only ever spotted in ones and twos populated the landscape in herds. It felt like getting something back that I didn't know I'd lost—finding a home that I never knew I had.

I began to set out on foot, backpack in tow, into this wild landscape, hoping to learn more intimately the roadless portions that inspired Aldo Leopold generations earlier. It was on one of those early backpack trips in the mid- to late-1990s that I inadvertently discovered how nature intended a ponderosa pine forest to look. I was packing south from Willow Creek into the Gila River headwaters when I came upon a prescribed fire around Turkey Feather Pass. The blaze was burning so predictably that there wasn't even a crew watching over it. Like many areas deeper in the wilderness, the understory here had not been effectively fire suppressed. As a result, it had burned periodically, and huge centuries-old pines held up the sky like the pillars of a European cathedral.

At about one hundred years of age, a ponderosa's bark will begin the transition from black to a beautiful fire-resistant yellow. Many of these trees were so old that their bark was a seamless yellow plate of armor. I watched in amazement as fire crept calmly across the ground, occasionally torching a young black-barked ponderosa or a patch of Gambel oak, sparing the ancient yellow pines with just a bit of blackening to record the passage of flame. The ladder fuels and old grass were cleaned out, maintaining the forest's open structure. This was a *real* pine forest, I thought, not the overstocked, fire-suppressed groves I'd seen in the Jemez and Zuni Mountains.

I would carry that knowledge forward in my own forestry work. After AmeriCorps, I went to work for the experiential-education nonprofit Cottonwood Gulch Expeditions. As executive director, I was responsible for hundreds of acres of ponderosa forest around our base camp, the launch point for our youth trips into the Gila Wilderness. We began replacing the dog-hair pine thickets with more naturally spaced trees, and ultimately, as others continued that work, Cottonwood Gulch was able to reintroduce fire onto its property and to even use the location to train wildland fire crews.

IT WAS ALSO DEEP IN the Gila Wilderness that I would set a new course for my life. Shortly after 9/11, just as commercial jets began to take to the sky once again, I met up with an old friend from college, and we headed south and west from Albuquerque. It was early fall, and we passed through miles of yellow wildflowers, catching up on old times. I'd been doing a lot of thinking about where I was headed professionally, and it was on this trip that I'd find my new North Star.

We started, as I had before, at Willow Creek, backpacking across ranges and mesas with names like the Jerky Mountains and Jackass Park. We camped along the West Fork of the Gila

River under cottonwoods and Arizona sycamores and watched a billion stars pierce the black sky at night. We were treated to glimpses of elk and deer and the hoots of Mexican spotted owls. I emerged from that adventure with a lighter soul, and the following year, ran for Albuquerque City Council.

In my sixteen years of public service since then, the Gila landscape has remained my touchstone. In 2007, when my wife, Julie, and I were contemplating a congressional run in New Mexico's first district, we headed down to the Gila. Our older son, Carter, was still shy of his fourth birthday, and Micah was just months old, so our usual camping plans were replaced by day adventures to places like City of Rocks State Park and evenings spent in the historic Palace Hotel in Silver City or the Black Range Lodge in Kingston.

I'd stayed in Kingston many times for work and had learned to expect a large family of javelinas to show up at some point. Sure enough, late one evening, the barking of the local dogs let me know that a pack was making its way through town. I got up and looked outside to see roughly thirty javelinas foraging in the moonlight. Scooping Carter out of bed, I carried him outside in my arms. Javelina have very poor vision, and we were able to stand quietly and watch the animals go about their business. A group of javelina is called a squadron, and this one lived up to its name, noisily rooting about.

"What do javelinas do to little boys?" Carter whispered.

The javelina invasion entered our family lore, and Julie and I decided to embrace a congressional run that would dominate the next year and a half of our lives. Just a couple years later, Senator Jeff Bingaman would announce his retirement, creating an opening that allowed me to begin my work in the Senate.

I STILL RETURN TO THE GILA whenever I can, to cleanse my soul of the clutter and vitriol that infects so much of our politics today.

Sometimes I steal away between Christmas and New Year's to sleep in a wall tent and sit around a fire in the cold and quiet of this landscape that I love.

It was on one such trip that Carter harvested his first elk. He was twelve or thirteen, and we were camped at the base of a high mesa in the northern part of the Gila. We spent days patiently hiking up and down the piñon-covered hills and canyons before we spotted elk on a distant hillside one afternoon. It was close to sunset before we were able to approach close enough to hear the occasional limb break under the weight of a hoof. Unfortunately, we quickly realized, we had crept up on a small herd of cattle; the elk were further still.

Just minutes before the last shooting light, Carter spotted a cow elk with its head down grazing. It's one thing to be able to fire your rifle accurately at a target, and another thing altogether to harvest a living, breathing animal under stress and in fading light. I told Carter to take his time and settle his breath. He posted up on a bipod, trying to quiet the surging heartbeats and breaths that cause your rifle sights to move up and down in waves.

"If you feel confident in your rest and your shot, you can take it," I told him.

Carter clicked off the safety and squeezed the trigger.

After you fire a rifle, it's difficult not to lose the animal in the scope's field of view. Carter was immediately worried that he had missed. I knew from the sound that he had not, and together we hiked the last eighty yards to the fallen animal. I still have the photos of him with that elk, his face illuminated by headlamp and pride. The best memories, though, are of him learning how to respect and care for the meat this creature had provided us. His dedication in packing out the meat was matched by an enthusiasm for cooking it. For the next year, each dinner of "Carter's elk" was a trip back to the Gila, to memories of unending vistas and friends huddled around a woodstove while the mercury dipped outside.

AS THE WORLD HAS CHANGED, this place, remarkably, has remained wild and free. On our most recent family trip to the Gila, in 2019, my boys forded streams with walking staffs they'd made from the stalks of sotol plants and marveled at the strings of eggs left in the shallows by Woodhouse's toads. Julie and I watched as they explored a world frozen in time. They chased lizards, watched raptors wheeling above, and put away copious amounts of hot chocolate. Ancient pines stood watch over our campsites as Carter and Micah hung hammocks from these gently swaying giants. It was humbling to know that, according to the stories told by Geronimo, his cradle could have hung from these same swaying trees nearly two centuries ago.

This place, where I have sought refuge so many times in my life, is also a refuge for wild creatures, untamed streams, and the very idea of wildness. It is a living example of what we have lost across so much of our shared cultural landscape. A living, breathing place. Frightening one moment and tender the next, but never boring.

We are approaching the one hundredth anniversary of the idea, most notably articulated by Aldo Leopold, that this place deserves to exist on its own terms. It deserves to live on untamed and unbroken. My hope is that a hundred years from now, my generation will be remembered for being good stewards of this most radical idea. That we will have resisted the endless efforts to carve up, tame, dam, and defang this place of tooth and claw. That this Gila Wilderness will not be just a line on a map, but an idea still burning bright, like the light in the eyes of a wolf.

KARL MALCOLM

GILA ELEMENTAL

OUR REMAINING PLACES OF NATURAL DARKNESS DRAW a particular kind of refugee—the human inverse of moths seeking flame. While dark skies have grown rare elsewhere, the nighttime views over the Mogollon Range have become an attraction in and of themselves. The Cosmic Campground, near Glenwood, speaks to a growing recognition of southwestern New Mexico as a stargazer's mecca. Here in the Gila, the humility and internal reflection that are elusive under streetlights, or in the glow of our screens, are made available by the measure of our personal trivialities against an uncompromised night sky.

This bottomless backdrop was fully dimmed around a new September moon, lending added pop to the broad stripe of our galaxy arching horizon to horizon. I soaked in the Gila's unignorable skies despite being as cold, sore, thirsty, and spent as I could recall. I scooched the crescent of my body's front half as close to our small fire as possible without singeing myself. Our fire had become more than a source of light and warmth, as they always do. It was the center of our universe. I wrapped cold, stiff fingers around fire-heated chunks of igneous earth held in each sleeved palm, cradling my head on my elbow, and nodded in and out of sleep on a hard patch of uneven ground.

A good friend stoked the fire while I slept, each of us wordlessly rotating responsibilities in short, orbital intervals while we anticipated dawn. We had been on the move for twenty-four hours, a full planetary rotation, and had just shared the last of our water, doling out a couple of tablespoons each. When my turn to tend the fire came, I flexed and studied my knuckles, swollen and caked with dried blood from the last three-quarters of a mile we'd pushed through a ridgetop thicket of thorny New Mexico locust in the dying beams of our headlamps. Eventually, we were demoralized enough to surrender our efforts until the sun rose.

When he took back over with the fire, I rolled to face away from the flames to thaw my back, where the day's sweat had turned to accumulating frost. My breath steamed out into the darkness and I chastised myself for leaving my jacket behind when we cleared out our packs to minimize weight.

We had purged gear aggressively to make room for bulky loads of elk meat, which we'd been staggering under since hiking away from the spot where we had felled a bull late the previous afternoon. In his last hour of life, the bull had divided his attention between a harem of females and an equally matched competitor. With the two of them vying for breeding rights, it was possible for me to sneak from downwind into close shooting range for my bow and arrow.

After several hours of hard labor breaking down the immovable animal, the idea of being cold had seemed far-fetched. Despite knowing better, I'd intentionally dropped my jacket in the gear pile we amassed around the carcass for later retrieval. Our hope was that the human smells of our equipment would help keep bears, wolves, lions, and coyotes off the remaining meat until we could return.

Now the idea of warmth had become a fantasy. My friend nudged me awake to hear the wolves howling somewhere between our fire and our stash of gear and meat. The expanse of the Gila had humbled us again.

With my back to the fire, I faced my bulging pack and questioned whether I'd be able to lift it again at daybreak. I tried not to dwell on the two more round trips it would take to finish transporting a year's worth of food from the elk's body to our waiting coolers, still miles away. I pushed away nagging thoughts of how we were only halfway through our first load out. I closed my eyes and considered that many observers might view us as having remarkably strange ideas of what defines a good time.

The purity of my exhaustion was paired with an equal dose of appreciation—for wild animals, this place, a dedicated friend, the family I would feed back home, this small fire. A return to *Homo sapiens* basics. Simple but important things like night skies that remind me of my small place in all this vastness.

MY CHILDHOOD LANDSCAPES, in the beech and maple woods of Michigan's northwest lower peninsula, were, by comparison, not as wild. Few places are, of course. It was wild enough there, however, to rough-cut my personal definition of good times through immersive experiences with land in its raw form.

My brother and I were raised to recognize our good fortune in growing up in this special place, and it was easy to be thankful. I spent high school summers working as a first mate on a salmon boat fishing East Grand Traverse Bay. On land, we saw more wildlife than traffic. We had trout streams we could reach on foot, reliable morel hunting grounds, and forts in hidden spots we thought only we knew. The big skies over Lake Michigan pushed powerful storms ashore to wash clean our forests. The elements of earth, water, and air were there for us, unadulterated. We had our own small fires burning at the center of our universe. The life that sprang from our woods fed us, warmed us, and shaped who we would grow up to be.

Among our tools in that landscape was a rust-tinged cast-iron skillet. We kept it wrapped in a black plastic garbage bag and hidden in a log pile near a secluded stream. The skillet and nearby fire ring were as much a destination as the cold, clear water. With sleeping bags, a book of matches, a pocketknife, and a bottle of cooking oil, my brother, our friends, and I felt adequately prepared for the lives of mountain men. Never mind our general lack of mountains or, for that matter, legit facial hair.

In spring our camp menu would include trout. We'd keep the browns that met the state's eight-inch minimum while returning native brookies to their plunge pools and undercut banks. For measuring purposes, Dad cut us a length of shoelace at eight and a quarter inches, just to be sure. The leeks that filled the spring woods were an ideal addition, especially with wild fungi rounding out the dish. In early autumn, the camp menu might include black raspberries, crab apples, squirrels, rabbits, or, when we were lucky, a ruffed grouse. The ability to gather, catch, hunt, clean, cook, and eat over self-built campfires, without adult contribution or interference, was an important rite of passage.

In today's world, it will sound counterintuitive to some that a roving band of armed juveniles were staying out of trouble, rather than getting into it, but I can easily imagine the worse alternatives we might have pursued. My mom took a wise parental risk when I was in my mid-teens and particularly prone to raising hell. We made a deal that if I kept my grades up, she would let me choose one day each semester when she would call the front office at Glen Lake Community Schools and excuse my absence.

On those mornings I wandered the hills toward my stream and skillet in the first gray hints of dawn, while my schoolmates assembled under the sterile halogen beams of homeroom. My woods provided light and lessons of a different, and often more memorable, sort. I found newborn whitetail fawns, saw a redtail snag a screeching cottontail, installed a maple sap line, and had a flying squirrel land in my lap while I sat motionless awaiting the sun—all within walking distance of home.

Freedom in those woods put me on an early path to a conservation education, which eventually led me to the US Forest Service, and to the Gila, which I would quickly come to recognize as one of the crown jewels of our nation's public lands.

I WAS IN GRADUATE SCHOOL when I planned my last overnighter to my hidden skillet and stream. The idea was to look for trout and wild turkeys during a three-day weekend back home in late April. But I was caught off guard when I came upon an unfamiliar driveway. A house had popped up where previously morel mushrooms had done the popping. My fire ring was grown over, nearly imperceptible, and too close to someone's yard to be a suitable camping spot. The homeowners must have had kids because they had installed a trampoline. It sat near the place where I had missed a shot at a deer when I was still too young to drive a car. The log pile and skillet were long gone.

I abandoned my plans and instead studied the land-ownership plat book to make sense of what had happened during my time away at college. The landscape was a patchwork of public land and privately held woodlots. Growing up, I'd spent long summer days helping bale hay, mill lumber, split firewood, repair barns, and look after livestock for surrounding landowners. With the permissions that hard work engendered, I never had to pay much attention to where one parcel ended and the next began.

The updated map made clear that my special spot now belonged to somebody whose name I did not recognize. Claims of eminent domain from formative childhood expeditions seemed unlikely to prevail in grown-up court. Rather than mounting a case, I hosted a one-man mental funeral for a place that had, without warning, been reduced to a bookended collection of memories of wild trout, sautéed mushrooms, cut feet, leaky tents, and a skillet I would never eat from again.

In comparing notes with others who are products of semiferal childhoods, I have come to know that many of us can quickly recall an influential wild place that has been tamed with startling speed, sometimes right before our eyes. Each of these places represents something sacred gone that will not be regained. By the simple laws of supply and demand, these losses underscore the increasing rarity, and the rising value, of those places retained in a natural state.

THE GILA WAS ENVISIONED to be such a place. Its wildfires still burn at scales largely unimpeded by agency apprehension and public worries of homes or infrastructure being lost. Its native trout are still there waiting for cold-water currents to carry them their next dislodged stonefly nymph. Lesser known but no less noteworthy spikedace and loach minnow are in those streams too, with aquatic garter snakes and leopard frogs hunting along the banks and riffles. The raucous springtime whistles and hoots of Mexican spotted owls are commonplace, and at dawn, the birds trade calls with gobbling Merriam's turkeys, unaware that they are at the center of decades of debate about forest management under the auspices of the Endangered Species Act. Here the owls do not seem endangered. Mexican wolves course through the Gila's yellow-bellied ponderosas and ancient alligator junipers, keeping deer and elk forever on edge. It is easy to find trees predating America. When I sit at a likely vantage to search for elk or deer below, I find lithic flakes at my feet from like-minded predecessors who possessed skills in woodcraft that I can only superficially fathom. It is a place of steady persistence, a harbor from pervasive change.

Like our definitions of what constitutes a good time, the values we associate with our special places are largely subjective. My friends and I revel in the demands and misery of hunting and exploring deep in the Gila, where the bounds of our wandering are set by our physical capacity rather than by property lines. We find satisfaction in wild food that takes on deeper meaning through its source and our intense exertion in procuring it. The Gila provides respite and rewards to those willing to sweat and shiver.

In a broader sense, I value what the Gila Wilderness

represents. Beyond the achievement of 560,000 acres of wildlands conserved within its governmental boundaries, the Gila is symbolic of vision and forethought—a prophetic response to a timely recognition that we were, are, and always will be fundamentally constrained by what our living planet has to offer, and nothing more. The Gila is a product of pumping the brakes on environmental conquest before the need seemed existential.

In its rugged immensity, it reinforces through experience the simple truth that we hold a small and humble place *within* nature. Time here refreshes an awareness that we are cut from, part of, and dependent upon the elemental ingredients of natural systems. To those who listen, the Gila and its history remind us that there are no means of producing more of the precious, wild, raw materials underpinning every breath and heartbeat.

As an ecologist, I appreciate the Gila as a haven for unique southwestern biodiversity molded by time and place. Pragmatically, I think of the water that flows from these mountains to dependent faucets downstream. At a personal level, I treasure places and animals I can both cherish and believe immune to the further spread of roads and all that they bring. As a father, husband, brother, son, and friend, I value the deep connections to people I love, strengthened and enriched through our shared experiences in wild places.

Perhaps above all, I appreciate the reframing of perspective that comes in the Gila, where personal strains and ego are recalibrated by the infinite dark sky. The landscape has the same boundless feel as the small fire I am curled around, absorbing its warmth and light. When the sun's return dims the Milky Way and brings first light to the Mogollons, I am brought back to the level of self, with a resharpened awareness that I am an infinitesimal piece of a truly big place.

PAM HOUSTON

ON (NOT) WANTING TO SEE A WOLF

THE UNITED STATES IS A COUNTRY OF 330 MILLION PEOple and we own, collectively, almost half a billion guns, including the fifty million new ones purchased since the beginning of 2020. In the Rio Grande National Forest, which surrounds my home in Colorado, I can no longer go for a day hike without hearing the report of a rifle. This was always the case during hunting season, but last summer solstice a volley of bullets whizzed past me and the dogs as we were hiking up Ivy Creek Road. On Thanksgiving Day, a couple of shooters had brought along enough ammunition to provide the soundtrack for an entire three-hour hike up Farmer's Creek, and on Christmas Day, in Seepage Creek Canyon, we watched a young man with a handgun unload hundreds of rounds of bullets into the thin layer of ice that covered the reservoir.

But this is not an essay about gun culture, or lead poisoning of the national forest, or even Colorado, not exactly. It is an essay about the Mexican gray wolves who have been reintroduced to a portion of their original homelands, including the Gila Wilderness and the Gila National Forest in New Mexico. These small wolves, also known as lobos, have been brought back in hopes of reawakening the elk to their own natural instincts as prey, forcing them to keep moving along the riparian areas and thereby improving the biodiversity, not just along the river bottom but throughout the ecosystem, a strategy that's been extremely effective in Yellowstone National Park.

The wolves' presence in the Gila, however, is tenuous and conditional. It demands that the wolves understand the difference between killing an elk calf and a cow's calf, on understanding the boundaries of grazing allotments, even though the cows keep moving around. It demands they stay out of trouble, even though many of the ranchers continuously and intentionally make trouble for them. It demands they mind their wolf p's and q's.

It was those same ranchers and their forbearers, along with a predator-control task force and more than a few randos who like to drive around the forest and blow living things away, who, by 1970, had reduced the entire worldwide Mexican gray wolf population to seven. A binational alliance between the US and Mexico rounded those stragglers up and put them in a captive breeding program so the species would not be lost for all time. In 1998, the US Fish and Wildlife Service began reintroducing wolves to the Gila, the ultimate goal a vibrant, secure, and healthy population of 750 wolves. But not everyone in the Gila is in favor of the program, and in the nearly quarter century since that first release, individual wolves have been leg-trapped, bludgeoned to death with a shovel, hit by speeding vehicles, removed for cattle predation, relocated back to captivity, and shot for no apparent reason at all. Yet somehow, in spite of that, their numbers have grown, slowly, shakily, to 186.

Now I was going to the Gila to see the wolves. I love encountering wildlife and canids most of all. To see a wolf bound across the trail in front of me, to hear them howl together in the middle of the night would restore something essential in me that 2020 had taken. But I also didn't want to see the wolves, because if I saw the wolves it would mean they were allowing themselves to be seen, and if they were allowing themselves to be seen, they might be seen by those who wanted to kill them.

So many beautiful beings died in 2020. In my immediate circle, two friends to COVID and two more to suicide. Thirty-six hundred doctors and nurses, countless elders, children, schoolteachers, grocery clerks. Wolf puppies bludgeoned in their dens, bear cubs likewise, millions of birds lost to methane, all the skinny whales—so much suffering, all at the hands of the same insidious and implacable machine. Something primal in me recognized that if a wolf were to be shot before my eyes in the Gila, if my presence might have caused her to redirect her path into the path of a bullet, it might also be the death of me.

A FEW MONTHS BEFORE the 2020 election, I began receiving death threats via social media. I am an increasingly outspoken woman, and I'm told by people who have been at activism longer than I have that death threats not only come with the territory, they're proof I'm on the right track. I have a recurring dream so often it's hard not to consider it premonition. I open my eyes and out my bedroom window is a pasty man with a chin beard and tiny receded eyes lifting a rifle to his shoulder. He is standing in my driveway, taking aim, and I know the bullet is going to come through my window, shattering the glass and hitting me right between the eyes.

AS WE DRIVE INTO THE GILA, in this, the twentieth consecutive year of drought (qualifying, now, as megadrought), the word that leaps to mind to describe the landscape is *hammered*. The cows have turned former meadows into sand pits. There's so little left for them to eat they cluster in the paltry shade of trees from which they have stripped most of the branches. It looks like sub-Saharan Africa, like it hasn't rained in a century. When we climb a hill into a remnant forest, most of the trees on both sides of the road are marked with fluorescent paint for a timber sale. In the wake of 2020, I'm not sure whether I feel like one of those parched and exhausted cows, or a dust-covered ponderosa, or more like the cow-pied, sunburnt, and sand-blasted landscape itself.

We disperse camp on the highest ridge we can drive to—a little less desiccated—though a recent wildfire has turned most of the trees into hoodoos. We are not out of the car five seconds when I hear the first gunshots. Target practice, it sounds like, but too close for me to relax. I never really relax about bullets anymore. I walk across the road to pee, pick up a discarded beer can, and then five more, and then twelve individual plastic water bottles somebody couldn't bother to haul out.

Madeleine Carey, WildEarth Guardians' greater Gila Guardian and expert on the captive breeding program, the Gila River, Forest Service policy, every single nuance of New Mexico's public lands, and our tour guide here in the Gila, fills us in on the success of the cross-fostering program (in which biologists smuggle genetically favorable puppies into the den of an already nursing wolf—imagine waking up and realizing you had three more kids than you thought!), on grazing leases that may be retired in the near future, on the difficulties of catching ranchers and others who are harming wolves illegally.

Night has fallen over our campsite when suddenly Maddie looks over her shoulder and says, "Hey you guys, there's a wolf right over there."

And sure enough, there is a canid trotting through the center of our campsite. She moves like a ghost dog, silent, light-footed. She's within fifty feet of us and not making a sound. Backlit by moonlight, it's impossible to say for sure, wolf or coyote. As she completes her circle around us and trots into darkness, I feel relief wash through me. If she is a wolf, no one is going to see her tonight but us.

HALFWAY THROUGH 2020 I RENTED a condo in Santa Fe, a place to flee not just the guns, but also those who swore George Soros made COVID in his basement, those who called me a name every time I entered the post office wearing a mask.

On an early October evening I was heading back to Colorado on 285 through the San Luis Valley past a hundred houses flying Trump flags and billboards. Many of those houses still fly them today. I was in my Prius, had safely navigated the wildlife corridors on the New Mexico side of the border before dusk, but now, just south of La Jara, it was nearly dark. Then there were headlights, brights and yellow fog lights, much too close in my rearview, the sound of a mufflerless diesel filling the car. I could make out three men, two large and one emaciated, but the headlights obscured more details than that. They fell back for a second and revved up again, this time nearly kissing my bumper.

As in farm country everywhere, the roads were a grid that I knew well. I took my first left, suddenly, with no turn signal, and they came right with me. As they rounded the corner, I saw the truck was flying, in total, five Trump flags, including an oversized one, wedged to sail over the entire bed. Up and back, up and back; this time their truck did touch my bumper. I looked for a farmhouse: there were Amish back there who I thought might be pacifists. Did I want to commit myself to an actual driveway? What if no one was home?

Kenny Chesney blared from the truck, loud enough to hear even through my closed windows. I took a right, onto an even smaller road, and they stuck to my bumper around that corner too.

This is how it all ends, I thought. Like an aging she-wolf, I had stumbled onto the allotment that belonged to the Trump supporters of the San Luis Valley, had been foolish enough to drive my fuel-efficient vehicle, which I knew posed an immense moral threat to their souls. I had not minded my progressive p's and q's and now I would be trapped, or relocated, put into a cage as a cautionary tale to others, perhaps shot and strung up by my hind feet.

The road turned into dirt. Ahead was a little grain silo,

nothing more. I pulled over and flipped my hazards on. I looked briefly around the car for something I could use to defend myself (a cold bag of organic groceries? jumper cables?), opened the door, and threw myself toward them, empty-handed but for the force of my rage. They'd pulled in right behind me, but I could tell by their faces they'd not expected a confrontation, perhaps thinking I'd sit inside my Prius forever, waiting for them to decide whether or not to let me live.

"What the *f---* is your problem," I shrieked, prepared to annihilate them with my voice alone, to scratch their eyes out with my fingernails, but they were already out of the pullout and down the dirt road, flags flying, the words *f------ c---* drifting back to me on the wind. I stood still in the ensuing quiet and finally let myself shake, recognizing that I had been awakened to my natural instincts as prey. Had I thought of it, reader, I might have thrown back my head and howled.

ON DAY TWO, IN THE GILA, on an early morning game walk, I see a flash of a dog running up the hill ahead of us. "Wolf!" I blurt, though it could be anything. A tawny back, a light underside of a tail, a being light on its feet, and stealthy. Wolf? Coyote? Fox? Sometimes perspective can get squirrely in the big outdoors.

That night we are finished with dinner, ready to turn in, when a white diesel pickup pulls in a few hundred yards from our campsite, ostensibly looking for a flat place to park. Between the ranchers and the hunters and the loggers, this part of the national forest is nothing but a patchwork of roads and pullouts. There is absolutely no reason why these people, whoever they are, need to camp this close to us.

"I wonder if he knows we're here," I say, fear ramping up inside me from the sound of the diesel alone. There was a time, not very long ago, where I always, *always*, felt my very safest in the wild.

Maddie jumps up and rearranges her car so her headlights face his truck, then she turns on her high beams and returns to our little circle. The truck futzes around, making more ruts in the forest duff for about ten minutes. Then it rumbles back out and drives away.

AMONG THE HARD TRUTHS OF 2020 is the understanding that when I go into the wilderness, I am not safe, anymore, from my own species, nor to the yoga studio, the grocery store, the movie theater, the nightclub, the church. And I am a white woman. Take a moment to consider how much more hunted I would feel if I were Black, or Indigenous, or Asian, or identifiably queer. In the binary that is currently the United States of America there are only two categories, hunter and hunted. I want there to be wolves in the Gila, but I want them to be invisible. As I myself want to be invisible. It is the only way either of us will survive.

On the last morning in the Gila we hike into the canyon of the Middle Fork, below Snow Lake, the water making it lush, by Gila standards, paradisiacal. On the way back we see a canid trotting down to the reservoir to get a drink and when he sees us approaching, rather than slinking away, he stands tall, in a kind of a challenge.

Wolf, we think, surely, and though he's a long way across the water, we move out to the end of a boat ramp to get as close as we can. My husband, Mike, is behind us with his camera and his long wildlife lens. The dog drinks, watching us, drinks again, then runs to the top of a little ridge and faces us, another challenge. No coyote I know has anything like that much hubris.

Mike zooms in, and even on his camera's tiny digital screen the too-pointy face and too-pointy ears are unmistakable. Not a wolf after all, but a coyote, if one who seems to be taking his social cues from the wolves.

"Poor coyotes," Maddie says. "Nobody is ever happy to see them."

"I am," I say, and it's true. Because in spite of my trepidation, it still does my soul good to see any canid, any wild thing, any being who is constantly hunted and is managing, anyhow, to survive.

SEEDS 100

"I can tell you that a diversion is expensive. People around me have all told you. I can tell you that a diversion would be harmful to the environment. I can tell you that it is a poorly thought-out plan…. I can tell you that the alternatives would preserve one of the most beautiful rivers in New Mexico. And I can also tell you that I am the future. That I am a young person, and I am going to have to live in a world that is created by your decisions."

—Ella Jaz Kirk (1999-2014)
Testimony to the New Mexico State Legislature, February 13, 2014

GABE VASQUEZ

EL OSO

D ID ANYONE EVER TEACH YOU HOW TO HOLD A CRAW-
fish without getting pinched? How about a hell-
grammite? And if so, did they teach how to find
these larvae, capture them, and use them for bait?
The natural world has much to offer us humans if
we make the time to explore it and, more importantly, to protect
it after we unlock its secrets.

The Gila is one of the world's greatest natural wonders, the
nation's first designated Wilderness, home to incredible biodiversity, history, culture, and people. It represents the abundance
of desert riches for us to enjoy and help care for here in southern
New Mexico.

If we're lucky and privileged, we learn those lessons when
we're young. But the majority of New Mexicans don't, and that's
an injustice on its own. Wild places like the Gila, and all their
gifts, are often reserved for those with the economic means, the
physical ability, and the experience it takes to get there. But mentorship and companionship may be the most important keys to
access.

Just ask thirteen-year-old Jose of Anthony, New Mexico. On
a warm spring morning Jose woke up to walk around camp in
the Cliff-Gila Valley. A collection of fifty-dollar tents flapped in
the breeze, encircling the remnants of the prior night's bonfire,
and two *discos* were already heated up and ready to receive a
healthy heaping of *chorizo con huevos* before a morning hike.
Jose nodded and smiled, giving thanks in his own way for

135

waking up to receive the world's greatest portable hiking meal, the breakfast burrito.

"Mister, what is this?" Jose asked. He pointed to a walking-stick cholla, admiring its radiant purple flowers as he called over a group of friends emerging from their tents to admire the long, spiny cactus.

I told Jose it was a cholla and told him it made one of the finest walking sticks around. He laughed and said, "Very funny." I pointed to a dead cholla stick under a tree, and replied, "Go get that—it's the same cactus you're looking at now. When they dry, they make for fine walking sticks—no needles. Go ahead, give it a try." A forest secret unlocked.

We would spend the next three days camping in the Gila Wilderness—nine youth from the Juvenile Community Corrections Program in Las Cruces, two adult chaperones, and two volunteers from the Nuestra Tierra Conservation Project, which works to ensure that people from *frontera*, or border, communities have access to the outdoors.

We learned about the proposed Gila River diversion, about the native and invasive plant and aquatic species of the Gila, what to do if we encountered a black bear or a mountain lion (that was a popular question), the differences between wilderness and forest land, the Native peoples and cultures of the Gila, and so much more.

We fished for catfish, bass, and Sonoran suckers at Turkey Creek. We caught crawfish and hellgrammites at the Gila Box campground in Cliff. We poked a dead egret with a stick at Bill Evans Lake. We swam in the Gila River and jumped into swimming holes from magnificent sandstone cliffs. We stayed up telling ghost stories and making late-night tacos, and for the first time for many of these youths, we saw the Milky Way in all its glory. Of course, the youth also eagerly explored every mountaintop surrounding camp to see if they could get cell phone service (they couldn't).

For these young people, whose upbringing was filled with conflict and trauma, unlocking the secrets of the Gila Wilderness was more than just a trip to the forest. It was an opportunity to see the world in a different way. Among the many benefits that the Gila provides, its impact on our mental health and our understanding of ourselves is one of the most important.

You see, the Gila is more than spiraling mountain chains dotted with aspen and Douglas fir. It is more than its lowlands, with juniper, oak, and cactus. It is even more than one of the last free-flowing rivers in the Southwest, and more than the nation's first Wilderness. It's a place where we, its visitors, inhabitants, and admirers, can better understand our place in the world, and where we can develop a genuine appreciation and conservation ethic for all things wild.

MY LATE GRANDFATHER JAVIER BAÑUELOS—or, as his friends called him, El Oso—first taught me that the wild lives inside us. Having moved from the rancho in El Remolino, in the Mexican state of Zacatecas, to Ciudad Juárez, he carried the spirit of the outdoors and the lessons it taught with him always, despite making his living as a mail carrier and TV repair man. He took me out of the crowded, polluted, and industrialized city center and into some of the most beautiful grasslands and mountain ranges in Chihuahua and the Sierra Madre, where he taught me how to fish and pointed out wildlife as we drove through winding forest roads. It was these early experiences that helped shape my values and my care for the natural world.

I've been lucky since then to have had many mentors, guides, and unlockers of secrets in the Gila. Ray Trejo, former Deming Public Schools assistant superintendent, took me on my first turkey hunt in the Black Range, teaching me how to look for signs of the birds, and, eventually, how to call them in. Andrew Black, a Presbyterian minister from Santa Fe, taught me how to fly-fish, skills that led to landing my largest smallmouth bass on a black wooly bugger on the East Fork of the Gila. I had the opportunity to meet the late Dutch Salmon, and to hear his stories, just a year before his passing. Locals like Patrice Mutchnick, Allyson Siwik, and Donna Stevens—who have dedicated their careers to protecting the Gila—showcase its beauty and majesty to anyone who asks, myself included.

Outdoor mentorship is offered in many ways—through nonprofit programs, school-based programs, state and federal programs. All these opportunities should be fully funded, and should specifically target low-resourced youth, families, and communities. Because if we are truly to say these are our public lands, they must be made public and accessible to *everyone.*

And this is happening. Programs like New Mexico's Outdoor Equity Fund have already provided grants to organizations, including some in Grant County, to purchase the gear and hire the guides to take more of our youth into the Gila. At the national level, federal programs like Every Kid in a Park, the Outdoor Recreation Legacy Partnership Program, the Urban Waters Federal Partnership Program, and the Urban and Community Forestry Program are all helping to get a more representative population of young people outdoors.

BEFORE NEW MEXICO'S STATEHOOD, before Manifest Destiny, and long before the mining boom, the Gila was home to the Mogollon, Ancestral Puebloan, Apache, and other Native people—many of their stories, dwellings, and artifacts remain imprinted as petroglyphs and safeguarded inside dwellings, arroyos, canyons, and the river itself. But these are not people of the past—they are very much of the present. Their descendants live here today. The Gila is not their ancestral land; it is, in fact, still their land, and the next one hundred years of the Gila should reflect and honor this.

When youth like Jose hear stories about the Indigenous history of this special place, their eyes beam; they want to hear more. They want to see the dwellings, and they want to know about the cultures who built them. It is through this experience that the Gila again becomes a teacher, not just of natural knowledge, but of the nature of humans, and what we must do to be better people, better caretakers of the land and of each other.

The future of the Gila must reflect, honor, and embrace this history in effective ways—in every aspect of education, signage, and storytelling across the national forest, not just at the Gila Cliff Dwellings visitor center. Similarly, the opportunities to tell those stories, to provide those guided outings, to work within our federal land management agencies, should be afforded to the Native peoples whose home this is.

We must do better, too, for every young person like Jose, who might never in his life have seen the Gila—a place just two and a half hours away from his home—if it weren't for dedicated mentors and the Nuestra Tierra program.

The next hundred years of the Gila should be just as much about people as about conserving water, wildlife, and landscapes. Communities must all work together to ensure that the Gila is a welcoming place to all, and that it inspires future generations of New Mexicans to enjoy, love, and care for these special places.

MARTHA SCHUMANN COOPER

THE LAND LOVES US BACK

WAITED AT THE EL PASO AIRPORT FOR MY DAUGHTER MOLLY TO
arrive. We first met when she was eighteen, but I have always
known her, the memory of her dark serious eyes gazing up
at me after her birth, her perfect full lips and scrunched-up
eyes, the softness of her brand-new skin, her silky newborn
hair. That summer after Molly's birth I could not bite into an
apricot. I rubbed my thumb against the baby-soft fuzz of its skin,
and tears slid down my cheeks.

What could be more unnatural than a mother giving away
her baby? Twelve years after Molly was born, I wondered about
this as I breastfed my daughter Frances. Sitting with my warm,
naked child pressed against me, I thought of Mary Oliver writing, "You only have to let the soft animal of your body love what
it loves." My husband, Tomás, and Frances and I live in a valley
where the Gila River is mostly diverted to grow grass for cattle.
Through the open bedroom windows, I listened to the mournful
wailing from the mama cows in the days after their calves were
separated from them and sent away in trucks. I wept, holding
Frances nursing at my breast, thinking of Molly, too, remembering my hot, achy, and swollen breasts in the days after Molly was
born, the emptiness and grief that filled those days and so many
afterwards.

I wonder about the ways we recover, or not, from the trau-
mas our bodies carry, and how we carry them in our bodies
and hearts. What happens when we can't love what we love?
Still today, whenever I feel Frances's small, warm, strong hand

holding mine as we walk the dirt roads on the farm where we live, my breath catches. This is what love feels like.

MOLLY FIRST VISITED ME IN 2017, during her January break from college in Alabama. Just days before she arrived, Frances and Tomás and I had slept out in a field by the river, by a favorite old log sculpted by river and wind and sun and delivered by flood. We'd piled together in our sleeping bags, with a big down comforter on top, on a deep night full of bright stars, frost settling onto our cheeks and noses and hair. When Molly arrived, she wanted to sleep out in the cold, too. We loaded up gear in backpacks; she liked the feel of the pack on her body. We walked approximately five hundred feet through the yard, over the ditch, and out into the hay field and slept next to each other; I mere inches away from this baby girl of mine. I woke early to the sound of sandhill cranes in the field and gazed in the dawn light at still-sleeping Molly, buried beneath the covers with a wool hat barely on her head. I extracted myself and walked to the house to make hot tea, which I brought out to the field, tiny ice crystals on the grass shimmering in the morning light.

Maybe it was the feel of the backpack, maybe the stars, maybe it was the tea. But Molly said she wanted to go backpacking for real. So on this hot August day in 2019, she was flying into El Paso.

We spent the night before our trip at the Wilderness Lodge in Gila Hot Springs; a group of Tomás's and my close friends were stretched across the wide porch, a cooler of beer nearby, snacks on a table. I introduced Molly as my daughter, which prompted looks of confusion and curiosity. As we settled into easy conversation on the porch, Jane, soul mother of the Gila Hot Springs community, asked in a kind and direct way, "What's the story?" I shifted closer to Molly sitting beside me. We had not prepared to tell this story of relinquishment and loss and love over cocktails, so we offered the short version: how I had chosen Molly's parents, how we'd talked regularly over the years, how Molly and I had become pen pals seven years ago. Someone said, "Hey! It's like a *This American Life* story!"

No one asked us the hard questions, out of kindness and politeness; no one asked the question that dogged me for years: Why did I give my baby away? How could I do it? I had simple answers I had turned over in my head, focused on scarce resources and lack of support. But after meeting Molly when she was eighteen and returning home—filled with fresh grief, riffling through old journals and letters, my pant legs soggy with tears—I understood how broken I had been when I had her. I'd experienced a breakdown after college, catalyzed by military-style Peace Corps training, and it had destroyed my sense of self, the way I knew my way in the world. Still emerging from the darkest days of my life, I could not imagine a path towards being the parent I wanted for this small being in my belly.

That evening at the Wilderness Lodge, as the sun dipped below the ridge to the west, Molly and I looked at the map, discussing routes and rain and the unlikely possibility of the river rising. We settled on a simple out-and-back route up the West Fork; my goals were merely for Molly to enjoy her first experience backpacking, and to be near water.

As the light faded, she and I slipped into the hot springs. I had worried briefly about this, knowing that stripping down was not part of Molly's family culture. But she took to naked soaking and basking like she had grown up a Gila hippie. My girl, formed in my body, who credits her long and strong legs to me but grew up so far away, was quick to decide that she too was a "Gila woman," strong and beautiful.

We slept that night in my friend Jon's little one-room studio—me on the futon, Molly on thick sleeping pads on the floor. My old dog Tessa was on the rug. I awoke after some initial hours of sleep and, after a while, sensed that Molly was awake too.

"Should I read aloud to us?" I ventured to ask. Within the bubble of light created by my headlamp, I read Robin Wall Kimmerer's essay "Epiphany in the Beans," describing the miracle of raising food and connecting with the earth. Eventually we slept.

WE MADE OUR WAY UP the West Fork the next day, slopping slowly through countless creek crossings, pausing to notice giant sycamores and their bone-like branches reaching for the sky, their hand-shaped five-pointed leaves. I said something about the bean essay. I have a deep fondness for growing green beans, a powerful local pole-bean variety, on elaborate forts constructed of bent and woven saplings. Molly shared her favorite line from the essay, the one I'd noticed, too: "The land loves us back."

We camped that night above the West Fork, high enough to catch some morning sun. I wasn't surprised to discover shards of elaborately painted pottery, evidence of ancient people once inhabiting this knoll, perched safely above the floodplain but with easy access to water. Often when I camp in the Gila, I find that I've settled on the same flat, elevated areas where people lived long ago.

In the morning, I pulled out the trail map, trying to sort out our actual location relative to all the bends of the river. Molly pointed out the label for the Gila Wilderness, and I explained that wilderness with a capital *W* is a federally protected place where motors and bikes and chainsaws, humans with noisy toys, are excluded. A place where fires and floods persist, the whole broad spectrum of destruction and creation. This river, this place, that I love.

At our campsite we were surrounded by ponderosa pines and oaks, the forest gently sloping upward. I showed Molly deep fire scars from the 2011 Miller Fire etched on the base of trees, a living, seared record. The Gila is a place where large fires move across the landscape at a rate that approaches their historical frequency, a place where fire is allowed to love the land, and where the health of the land depends on this love.

I moved to New Mexico after graduate school, after Molly was born, the fall before the 2000 Cerro Grande Fire tore through the Jemez Mountains above Los Alamos, the megafire that began an era of megafires. During the span of Molly's life, the scale and intensity of fires has dramatically increased. I am intrigued by how landscapes and rivers respond to disturbances and how they recover, how they can change in irrevocable ways: forests to shrublands, rivers to reservoirs.

Canyon wrens—new friends to Molly—offered songs to us in the mornings and evenings. From our campsite, we listened to water moving around and over rocks and logs. We discovered the nest of a handsome black spider in rocks at the river's edge where I sat perched pumping water. As we hiked up the West Fork, I pointed out clumps of grass and sticks stuck to the trunks and branches of trees, visible markers of the height of the most recent flood. We paused to notice mushrooms. Molly had spent the spring semester of college in Ireland, studying art and attempting to make mushroom prints—carefully breaking the cap off and pressing the delicate gills onto paper. In spite of the regular rain there, she found few mushrooms, so she was delighted to find gold and brown and speckled mushrooms here in the damp earth. I was introduced to the idea of hiking as art project as she added prints to her journal, some inky with delicate thread-like lines, others pale and smeary.

We gathered flowers as we walked, adorning Molly's head with a crown of every color and shape: dark purple larkspur, pink wild geranium, orange globemallow, lavender bergamot, red Indian paintbrush, yellow monkeyflower from the edge of the river, rainbow-petaled blanket flower.

Our conversation meandered. At one point I reflected that I seemed to have modest professional objectives, that though I was fiercely committed to conservation and equity, perhaps I wasn't *personally* ambitious enough. She said, "That's okay. We notice the small things." Why had that not occurred to me, that this is enough?

WEEKS LATER, HOME IN THE Cliff-Gila Valley, I was walking up the road towards the mighty Mogollon Mountains with my neighbor. She was describing her dark days of grief since losing her kind and sparkly-eyed husband, the great love of her life. She felt now just like she did when they fell in love, she said, consumed by intense and obsessive thoughts. What an unfair other side of joy, I thought, the depth of her grief as a measure of love.

Most relationships start with love and end with grief. With Molly, the two were intertwined from the beginning. Holding her in the hospital in the days after her birth, heart breaking, I cried until she cried too. Our relationship was defined by grief and loss from the very start, the emptiness only growing to create more of what I didn't have and could not hold. So now, this coming together after so many years, a great miracle of grief dissolving.

The day after our backpacking trip, back in Gila Hot Springs, Molly and I had made tea and walked out to watch the sun rise. I stacked two Paco pads on a lounge chair and settled in, making a place for my daughter to sit in front of me, using me as her back rest. The air was cool, and we pulled a blanket over us, sitting quietly as we watched the morning sunlight creep toward us on the grassy hillside to the west. A gray Townsend's solitaire with a round belly and slender tail perched in a nearby snag, also waiting for the sun to warm his fluffed-up feathers. I wrapped my arms around Molly's shoulders, my cheek leaning against her long, thick brown hair. I thought about our bodies laid bare to sun and water. The way bodies and places bear evidence of disturbances, our histories, bear testament to who we are. The stories we share of being broken and healed; of fire scars, flood debris, the forces that keep our forests and rivers whole, offering us mushrooms and flowers and canyon wrens. A river that flows freely, nourishing the landscape and people who swim in it, drink from it, and grow food with its water. Water that bears our weight when we surrender to it. This land shows us love, teaches us love, and loves us back.

RAMBLING

OVER THE COURSE OF A YEAR, MY DOG AND I RAMBLE IN Meadow Creek, in the Gila Wilderness.

To ramble (verb):

(1) walk for pleasure, typically without a definite route

(2) talk or write at length in a confused or inconsequential way

My dog is a catahoula-husky mix. She has a nose for dead things. She bites down on the corpse of a vulture and holds it for 0.8 miles, its black plumage jouncing in her mouth. She finds deer legs and dead rodents and carries them off like prizes.

What does the Gila tell us about death? Everything is recycled. Rotting logs teem with life: threadworms, beetles, hyphae, ants in bustling lines. The forest floor knows nothing of waste.

The sound of a crow protesting in the treetops. Now flying in divine circles. The circle is divine, is it not? Some say the triangle is divine, holy trinity and all. Some say the cross. For me it's the circle. Who draws perfect circles? Only geniuses, those touched by God. Giotto, Brunel, da Vinci.

When he was a child, da Vinci discovered a whale skeleton in a cave. From that moment, he became unceasingly curious about the world. He understood that the legend of the Creation was false; the universe was older and more mysterious than he'd been told. Those old bones turned da Vinci's life into a quest for truth.

My discoveries in the hidden places of the Gila are more modest: the shed skin of a snake, husky and brittle like burned paper, the silence of the moment after snowfall.

Trees have relationships. When one is withering, others can share their nutrients using an underground system that connects their roots. This process can revive ailing trees. Suzanne Simard, a Canadian ecologist studying in the forests of British Columbia in the early 1990s, discovered that even different species of trees share nutrients. She called this cooperative system "forest wisdom." When Simard published her findings in the journal *Nature* in 1997, the underground forest network was nicknamed "the wood-wide web."

The world's oldest tree is called Methuselah. It predates Jesus and Muhammad and the Buddha. It took root 4,850 years ago in the White Mountains of California.

The tree in front of me is of an unknown age. But from its twisted branches and wrinkled trunk I'll guess it was around when Shakespeare began writing his first sonnet.

Tree bark looks like alligator skin. Branches bend with the weight of fallen snow.

Of all the materials, wood is nature's masterpiece. Neither diamonds nor gold can match the grain of a pine tree stripped bare. They say diamonds are forever, but diamonds can't change. The timbre of a violin improves with age. Cellos resonate centuries after the maple is cut. Wood creaks and warps. A diamond only shines. It's a bauble, a pretender.

This tree has branches like an old lady's fingers. They are turned down, on display, as if she is showing me the wedding ring on her gnarled knuckles.

I come across an area of burned stumps, and trees toppled or collapsed on diagonals. What strange winds blew them down? I think of Hiroshima after the blast. I think of the word *holocaust*. Holocaust means "all burned."

A tremor in the undergrowth. A disturbance of some kind. Like an echo of distant explosions.

I realize, as my feet tread the path, that *I am* the disturbance. Whatever tranquility once lay here is now disrupted by my aesthetic gaze. Does the snake marvel at the beauty of the wilderness? Does the bear make metaphors of the river? Does the mountain lion stop to admire the mountain? I'm the intruder here.

To wander (verb): walk or move in a leisurely, casual, or aimless way

To wonder (verb): desire or be curious to know something

In greek mythology, Zeus was so moved by the weeping of the mother Niobe, who'd lost seven sons and seven daughters, that he turned her into a rock. From this rock flowed a never-ending stream of water. This was how the ancients represented pain.

I watch the water sweep down from the rocks after a spring rain. The water knows nothing of Niobe's agonies. But it has memory. Water remembers where it came from. That's why there are floods. The water is reclaiming its old territories, making good on a promise.

In Europe, when the water levels drop, hunger stones appear. They are hundreds of years old, and they are warnings, end-of-days messages. One hunger stone in the Czech Republic reads "Wenn du mich siehst, dann weine." *If you see me, weep.*

The English poet Philip Larkin wrote, "What will survive of us is love." According to Robert Macfarlane, he was wrong; what will survive of us is plastic. My fellow ramblers have seen fit to leave a baby's drinking bottle, the barrel of a Nerf gun, sandwich packaging (chicken mayo), a toy soldier, several plastic bags, a roll of Scotch tape, a Coca-Cola bottle (empty), a toddler's pink shoe, and a red bucket. Even my dog turns up her nose. These are gifts from the modern world to the old. Offerings to the goddess of nature from us, the scourge.

Rilke: "Beauty is fundamentally tied to trauma and terror." I marvel at the vista. Green swaths for miles on miles, hills that fade, become indistinguishable from the sky. But the terror is always here. The unknown. That's why they set fairy tales in the woods.

When I walk through Meadow Creek, I think of the French composer Olivier Messiaen. I try to hear what he heard.

In 1940, Messiaen was captured and sent to a German POW camp. There, he listened to the songs of blackbirds and nightingales. He transcribed them and used them to write "Quartet for the End of Time." The piece was performed in the prison camp, with Messiaen on piano and fellow prisoners on clarinet, violin, and cello. After his release, Messiaen spent the next forty years wandering across France to listen to birds. Sometimes he slept rough. By the time he died he'd composed hundreds of pieces based on birdsong. He experienced synaesthesia, which means he associated sounds with color. He once said the song of a rock thrush was the same hue as the bird's orange breast. He likened E major to sunset red.

It's coming from the treetops. Birds warbling. Staccato peeps. Chirps and trills. One sings something like an arpeggio. My dog barks a response. She's been touched by the Messiaenic muse.

Birds sing to warn away predators and to attract mates. Male birds sing more than females. Sometimes male and female birds sing duets. The male brown thrasher knows around two thousand songs. Some bird species are experts in mimicry. One type of Scottish starling can reproduce the sound of a sheep. Another type of city starling can mimic buses.

When Darwin's theories were being used as evidence that competition drives evolution, the future Russian revolutionary Kropotkin traveled fifty thousand miles on horseback through Siberia. He studied migrating birds, fish, mammals, and insects, and discovered that the defining trait of the beasts in their natural habitat was cooperation, not competition.

And thus birds sing duets.

Geronimo said, "Nothing survives but the rock." We say rock face. The rock has a face. It is square-jawed and flat. It expresses nothing. Around me the leaves shiver in the breath of the wind.

The cave of Er Wang Dong in Chongqing, China, is so large it has its own weather system. From observing this cave, the locals are able to predict the weather. When they see fog drifting out, they know rain is coming.

I get caught in a storm. The rain batters the trees like bullets. I stand under a ponderosa pine and watch the path turn into a river.

In 2020, reindeer herders in the Russian Arctic discovered in the permafrost the perfectly preserved carcass of an Ice Age cave bear. Its soft tissue and internal organs, teeth, nose, and fur were still intact. Scientists estimate that the bear lived between 22,000 and 39,500 years ago.

Bear sightings in this part of the Gila are rare. Rare bears. They are understandably shy. We have the guns.

My dog metamorphoses in the Gila. At home she's a puppy, content to gnaw a chair leg or two, dig a few holes in the backyard. Out here, she turns feral. Her ancestral instincts kick in. Nose to the ground, chasing hares, corralling deer, chewing bones. Red in tooth and claw. She doesn't want a cuddle or a caress; she wants meat. She wants a fight to the death.

Roots erupt from the underland to trip me. I pick up a branch and use it as a walking stick. I could be Moses. My dog bounds ahead looking for wild things and carcasses, unhealed wounds.

EVE WEST BESSIER

GIBBOUS MOONS

Where were you marooned
when the desert bloomed
under a waning gibbous moon,
the prickly pear cacti
ripening like blood flowers
as late July rain,
settled and reflected
in impermanent pools?

Where did you bury your tears
when the last bald eagle
called over canyons,
speaking the old language
into a silence
deeper than instinct?

Where did you park
your past-due dream,
like an old Airstream
wilting in shimmering
steel and aluminum
by tattered cottonwoods
under midday sun?

The Gila cliff dwellers left
behind their mysteries
and their kitchens,
smoke-darkened ceilings
of dwellings where children
lay awake on winter nights

listening to coyotes sing
on mesa rims
under gibbous moons
growing into full,
or waning into the horns
of the bull

CONTRIBUTORS

ELIZABETH HIGHTOWER ALLEN is a contributing editor at *Outside* magazine and the founder of Hightower Creative, where she provides editing and consulting to publishers, magazines, non-profits, and individuals. She also serves on the Advisory Board of Writers on the Range. Her writing has appeared in *Outside*, where she wrote the Code Green environmental column, and the *New York Times* and *Washington Post* book reviews. Her editing work has been recognized by the National Magazine Awards, the Lowell Thomas Travel Journalism Awards, and the Best American Series. Originally from Nashville, Tennessee, she lives in Santa Fe, New Mexico with her husband and daughter.

JJ AMAWORO WILSON is the writer-in-residence at Western New Mexico University. His first novel, *Damnificados*, won four major awards and was an Oprah Top Pick. Another novel, *Nazaré*, came out in 2021. JJ has also written several books about language, two of which won awards that saw him honored at Buckingham Palace in 2008 and 2011. He has lived in Silver City, New Mexico, close to the Gila Wilderness, since 2008.

MICHAEL P. BERMAN wanders the terrain of the American West and Mexico Norteño. He was awarded a Guggenheim Fellowship in 2008 to photograph the Chihuahuan Desert for *Trinity*, the third book of a border trilogy with writer Charles Bowden. His most recent book, published by Museum of New Mexico Press, is *Perdido: Sierra San Luis*. His photographs are included in the collections of the Metropolitan Museum of Art, the Amon

Carter Museum, and the Museum of New Mexico. He has received grants for environmental work from the Lannan Foundation and the McCune Charitable Foundation, and the Governor's Award for Excellence in the Arts in New Mexico. Born in New York City, Michael lives in Silver City, New Mexico.

EVE WEST BESSIER writes poetry, essays and fiction. Her work is widely published, most recently in the *Los Angeles Review* and *El Palacio Magazine*, and has received literary awards. Eve is a poet laureate emerita of Silver City, New Mexico, and Davis, California. She is a retired social scientist and voice coach, and an avid nature enthusiast. Eve is a monthly columnist for *Southwest Word Fiesta* (www.swwordfiesta.org). Her published books include, *New Rain: a visionary novel*; *Roots Music: Listening to Jazz*; *Exposures: Tripod Poems*; and her latest release, *Pink Cadillacs: Short Stories*. Find out more at her website: www.jazzpoet-eve.com.

ALASTAIR LEE BITSÓÍ (Diné) is from the Navajo community of Naschitti, below the Chooshgai Mountains on the New Mexico–Arizona state line. The Southern Utah reporter for the *Salt Lake Tribune*, he has been an award-winning news reporter for the *Navajo Times* and communications director for the Indigenous-led land conservation nonprofit Utah Diné Bikéyah. His consulting business, Near the Water Communications and Media Group, trains media, nonprofits, businesses, and governments in cultural sensitivity. Alastair is co-editor with Brooke Larsen of the Torrey House Press anthology *New World Coming: Frontline Voices on Pandemics, Uprisings, and Climate Crisis*. He has a master's degree in public health from New York University College of Global Public Health and is an alumnus of Gonzaga University.

CHARLES BOWDEN (1945-2014) was the author of thirty-four nonfiction books, a contributing editor for *GQ*, *Harper's*, *Esquire*, and *Mother Jones*, a newspaper journalist whose main focus was the desert borderlands of the Southwest. He wrote eloquently about all the key issues—drug-related violence, illegal immigration, and the environment. Bowden's books include *Blue Desert*, *Blood Orchid*, *Killing the Hidden Waters*, *Some of the Dead are Still Breathing*, *The Sonoran Desert*, and *Blues for Cannibals*. A Pulitzer Prize nominee and winner of the 1996 Lannan Literary Award for nonfiction, he spent most of his life in Tucson, exploring the mountains and the desert he loved.

PHILIP CONNORS was born in Iowa, raised on a farm in Minnesota, educated at the University of Montana, and disillusioned by a stint in corporate journalism in New York. He is the author of three books: *Fire Season*, *All the Wrong Places*, and *A Song for the River*, from which "Birthday for the Next Forest" was adapted. His work has won the National Outdoor Book Award, the Reading the West Award for nonfiction, the Sigurd Olson Nature Writing Award, and the Grand Prize at the Banff Mountain Book Competition. He lives and works in the US/Mexico borderlands. This excerpt from *A Song for the River* (2018) appears courtesy of Cinco Puntos Press.

MARTHA SCHUMANN COOPER is the Southwest New Mexico program manager for the Nature Conservancy in New Mexico and has been blessed to live and work along the Gila River for the past fifteen years.

RENATA GOLDEN is a birder, naturalist, editor, and writer with an MFA in creative nonfiction from the University of Houston. Her essays have been published by *Terrain.org*, *About Place Journal*, *Creative Nonfiction/True Story*, and *Chautauqua*, among others, and in anthologies from Cornell University Press and Weeping Willow Books. She is currently at work on an essay collection about the Chiricahua Mountains titled *Mountain Time: Field Guide to Astonishment*. Originally from the South Side of Chicago, Renata lives in Santa Fe, New Mexico.

DEB HAALAND is the fifty-fourth US Secretary of the Interior. A member of the Pueblo of Laguna and a thirty-fifth-generation New Mexican, she made history when she became the first Native American to serve as a cabinet secretary. A single mother, Secretary Haaland put herself through college and ran her own small business, Pueblo Salsa, before serving as a tribal administrator at San Felipe Pueblo, and became the first woman elected to the Laguna Development Corporation Board of Directors and the first Native American woman to lead a state party. From 2019 to 2021, she represented New Mexico in the US Congress, where she focused on environmental justice, climate change, missing Indigenous women, and family-friendly policies.

JOY HARJO is the twenty-third Poet Laureate of the United States. A member of the Muscogee (Creek) Nation, she is the author of nine books of poetry, including the highly acclaimed *An American Sunrise*, several plays and children's books, and two memoirs, *Crazy Brave* and *Poet Warrior*. Her many honors include the Ruth Lily Prize for Lifetime Achievement from the Poetry Foundation, the Academy of American Poets Wallace Stevens Award, two NEA fellowships, and a Guggenheim Fellowship. She is executive editor of *When the Light of the World was Subdued, Our Songs Came Through—A Norton Anthology of Native Nations Poetry* and the editor of *Living Nations, Living Words: An Anthology of First Peoples Poetry*. She lives in Tulsa, Oklahoma.

MARTIN HEINRICH is a United States Senator for New Mexico. An avid sportsman and conservationist, Heinrich works to protect New Mexico's public lands, watersheds, and wildlife for future generations. Heinrich is the author and lead sponsor of the M.H. Dutch Salmon Greater Gila Wild and Scenic River Act. As a member of the Senate Energy and Natural Resources Committee, he has championed the designation of the Organ Mountains-Desert Peaks and Rio Grande del Norte National Monuments, passed legislation to establish White Sands National Park, and secured bipartisan support for the John D. Dingell, Jr. Conservation, Management, and Recreation Act and the Great American Outdoors Act, two of the most significant pieces of conservation legislation to be signed into law in decades.

PAM HOUSTON is the author of the memoir *Deep Creek: Finding Hope in the High Country*, *Cowboys Are My Weakness*, and other books. Co-author with Amy Irvine of *Air Mail: Letters of Politics, Pandemics, and Place*, Houston is the winner of the Western States Book Award, the WILLA Award for contemporary fiction, the Evil Companions Literary Award, and several teaching awards. She teaches in the Low Residency MFA program at the Institute of American Indian Arts and at University of California–Davis and is co-founder of the literary nonprofit Writing by Writers. She lives at nine thousand feet near the headwaters of the Rio Grande.

ELLA JAZ KIRK (1999-2014) was a determined activist who created a 6,400-signature petition that she delivered to New Mexico governor Susana Martinez to keep the Gila free of any diversion. Ella planned to earn a doctorate degree in aquatic ecology and apply her research to saving wild places. She died with two fellow high-school students while conducting aerial research on post-fire conditions in the Gila National Forest. The nonprofit Heart of the Gila (heartofthegila.org) celebrates her life and work, educating children, adults, and decision makers about the ecological, economic, and cultural values of rivers in New Mexico and the bioregions of the greater Southwest. Learn more at ellajazkirk.org._

PRIYANKA KUMAR is the author of the critically acclaimed novel *Take Wing and Fly Here* and she wrote, directed, and produced the award-winning feature documentary *The Song of the Little Road*, starring Martin Scorsese and Ravi Shankar. She is a recipient of the Aldo and Estella Leopold Writing Residency, an Alfred P. Sloan Foundation Award, a New Mexico/New Visions Governor's Award, and an Academy of Motion Pictures Arts and Sciences Fellowship. Her work appears in the *New York Times*, the *Washington Post*, the *Los Angeles Review of Books*, and *High Country News*. Her new book, *Conversations with Birds*, is forthcoming from Milkweed Editions.

ALDO LEOPOLD (1887-1948) was a conservationist, forester, philosopher, educator, writer, and outdoor enthusiast. Among his best-known ideas is the land ethic, which calls for an ethical, caring relationship between people and nature. A prolific author, Leopold conceived of a book, geared for general audiences, which would examine humanity's relationship to the natural world. Unfortunately, a week after receiving word that his manuscript would be published, Leopold died of a heart attack on April 21, 1948. A little more than a year after his death, *A Sand County Almanac* was published. It has since sold more than two million copies and been translated into fifteen languages.

KARL MALCOLM is a wildlife ecologist, conservation professional, public servant, and avid participant in the outdoors. He has worked for the US Forest Service in positions at local, regional, and national levels and taught internationally on conservation, fish and wildlife management, and wilderness stewardship. In addition to his peer-reviewed work, Karl has written for a variety of outlets including *Natural History Magazine*, *Backcountry Journal*, *MeatEater*, *Bugle Magazine*, the *Black Range Naturalist*, and *Pope and Young Ethic*. He resides with his wife,

Shoshona, and their children, Clara and Alexander in Cedarburg, Wisconsin.

BETO O'ROURKE lives in El Paso, Texas, where he and his wife, Amy, are raising Ulysses, Molly, and Henry in the historic Sunset Heights neighborhood. He has been a small business owner, a city council representative, and a member of Congress, representing Texas's sixteenth congressional district in the United States House of Representatives from 2013 to 2019. He currently leads Powered by People, which works to expand democracy and produce Democratic victories in Texas.

LAURA PASKUS is a longtime environment reporter based in Albuquerque, New Mexico. She is the environment reporter for New Mexico PBS and produces the monthly series *Our Land: New Mexico's Environmental Past, Present and Future*. Her book, *At the Precipice: New Mexico's Changing Climate*, was published in September 2020 by the University of New Mexico Press.

SHARMAN APT RUSSELL is the author of a dozen books translated into nine languages. Her *Diary of a Citizen Scientist* won the John Burroughs Medal for Distinguished Natural History Writing. Her *Within Our Grasp: Childhood Malnutrition Worldwide and the Revolution Taking Place to End It* combines her longtime interest in the environment and in hunger. Recent fiction includes the award-winning *Knocking on Heaven's Door*, an eco-sci-fi set in a Paleo-terrific future. Sharman lives in the magical realism of the Gila Valley, about a mile from the Gila National Forest.

JOE SAENZ is from the Warm Springs Band of Chiricahua Apache. His mother's peoples are the Huchiil, and his father comes from the Tci he nde, the Warm Springs Apache. He currently serves as council member of the Chiricahua Apache Nation. Mr. Saenz is the owner and operator of Wolf Horse Outfitters. He lives in his traditional territory, also known as Arenas Valley, New Mexico.

M. H. "DUTCH" SALMON (1945-2019) was an outdoor writer, publisher, and founder of High-Lonesome Books, a publishing company in Silver City, New Mexico. He was a conservationist, environmental activist, fisherman, homesteader, and author of *Gila Descending*, about his journey down the Gila River in 1983. He co-founded the Gila Conservation Coalition in 1984 to protect the free flow of the Gila and San Francisco Rivers, as well as the Gila and Aldo Leopold Wilderness areas. In January 2020, New Mexico senators Tom Udall and Martin Heinrich introduced the M. H. Dutch Salmon Greater Gila River Wild and Scenic Act to protect the Gila River.

JAKOB W. SEDIG is an archaeologist and postdoctoral research fellow at the Reich Laboratory of Medical and Population Genetics, Harvard University. His research focuses on the Mimbres region of southwest New Mexico, particularly concerning societal vulnerability and resilience during climatic downturns. His work also explores how to more fully integrate ancient DNA with archaeological studies and the ethical issues surrounding paleogenomic research. "Lessons in Resilience" was written on the ancestral lands of the Massachusett and Pawtucket people and is about the ancestral lands of modern New Mexico Pueblo and Apache people.

LEEANNA T. TORRES is a native daughter of the American Southwest, a *Nuevomexicana* who has worked as an environmental professional—from fish biologist to natural resources specialist—throughout the West since 2001. Her writing has appeared in such publications as *Blue Mesa Review, Tupelo Quarterly, Eastern Iowa Review, Minding Nature, High Country News*, and *High Desert Journal*.

TOM UDALL is a former US Senator from New Mexico and a life-long conservationist. Son of Stewart Udall, interior secretary in the Kennedy and Johnson administrations, he learned to love and value the land from a young age. Sen. Udall introduced legislation to include the Gila River under the Wild and Scenic Rivers Act and wrote or advocated for dozens of bills to move conservation forward, increase renewable energy, and combat climate change. He worked for two decades to increase funding for—and stave off cuts to—the Interior Department and the Environmental Protection Agency. He authored the successful 30x30 Resolution to Save Nature, setting a goal to protect 30 percent of lands and waters by 2030. His work culminated in President Biden promulgating a 30x30 Executive Order. Sen. Udall's leadership achieved two new national monuments in New Mexico—the Rio Grande del Norte National Monument and the Organ Mountains-Desert Peaks National Monument. In 2021, he was appointed U.S. Ambassador to New Zealand and Samoa.

GABE VASQUEZ is a first-generation American and the founder of the Nuestra Tierra Conservation Project. He is a city councilor in Las Cruces, New Mexico, an avid hunter and angler, a conservationist, and co-founder of the pioneering New Mexico Outdoor Equity Fund. He is a lifelong border resident and spends a large part of the year in the Gila National Forest. He is also a board member for the Outdoor Alliance and the New Mexico Division of Outdoor Recreation.

PRISCILLA SOLIS YBARRA is associate professor of Latinx Literature at the University of North Texas and senior fellow for the Study of Southwestern America at Southern Methodist University's Clements Center. Her first book, *Writing the Goodlife: Mexican American Literature and the Environment*, won the Thomas J. Lyon Book Award in Western American Literary and Cultural Studies. In 2016, she was an Aldo and Estella Leopold Writer in

Residence in Tres Piedras, New Mexico. She is also co-editor of *Latinx Environmentalisms: Place, Justice, and the Decolonial.* She lives on unceded Wichita and Caddo lands not far from where she was born, on the banks of the Trinity River, to a Mexican immigrant mother and a second-generation Mexican American father.

ACKNOWLEDGMENTS

MANY GENERATIONS HAVE WALKED THE Gila's trails before us, so it seems appropriate to first acknowledge them, from the Apache people who still care for this land to Aldo Leopold and his contemporaries, who had the foresight to set it aside. For decades, a wide-ranging group of environmentalists, forward-looking ranchers, and others have continued that work, including the dedicated staff ofAmerican Rivers, the Center for Biological Diversity, the Gila Conservation Coalition, the Gila Resources Information Project, NM Wild, the New Mexico Wildlife Federation, the Upper Gila Watershed Alliance, the Wilderness Society, and WildEarth Guardians.

This book is part of that tradition, a joint project of WildEarth Guardians and Torrey House Press. No one poured more love into it than Madeleine Carey, the organization's Greater Gila guardian, a tireless campaigner who hatched the original idea for the book. I'm also grateful to Leia Barnett, a passionate advocate who has proved a reliable lucky charm when you want to spot a Mexican gray wolf. Leia and Maddie, thank you for fielding all my ceaseless queries. I'd also like to thank WildEarth Guardians executive director John Horning and associate director Carol Norton for their decades of work on behalf of threatened species around the West.

I feel incredibly fortunate to be associated with Torrey House Press, which stands at the intersection of literature and conservation in the West. Torrey House's founder, Kirsten Johanna Allen, has served as my mentor and guide, providing wise edits and encouragement every step of the way. Creative director

Kathleen Metcalf did wonders with the cover and photographs, and Rachel Buck-Cockayne designed a fresh and powerful interior. Thank you to Anne Terashima, who not only saved me in copyedit, but organized the publicity for the book. I'm also grateful to Michelle Wentling for her patience in herding so many cats in event planning, and Maya Kobe-Rundio for the many hats they wore in creating this book.

First and Wildest would be far less beautiful without photographer Michael P. Berman's images. When I read his book *Gila*, I wondered how another anthology could measure up. But Michael was quick to donate not only a cover photograph, but all the photographs that enliven these pages. His essay is one of my favorites.

As for the other contributors, I am truly moved by their generosity. I'd particularly like to thank JJ Amaworo Wilson and Philip Connors, who led me to several of the writers represented here, and Alastair Lee Bitsóí, who not only worked with Joe Saenz to produce his powerful essay but provided cheerleading and moral support. A special thank-you to Tom Udall, for his wise foreword, and to Martin Heinrich, Beto O'Rourke, and Gabe Vasquez for their work protecting these lands and waters.

I owe a real debt to Buddy Huffaker, executive director of the Aldo Leopold Foundation, for his insights, and to Curt Meine for helping me navigate the Leopold Papers at the University of Wisconsin. I'm also grateful to Cynthia Bettison, Denise Chavez, Tom Fleischner, Patrice Mutchnick, Whitney Potter, Allison Siwik, and Veronica Tiller for their help and advice.

Every journalist needs a brain trust of their peers, and Mary Turner, Kevin Fedarko, Alex Heard, Abe Streep, Jonah Ogles, and Katie Arnold have served as mine. Thank you for still taking my calls. I'm also grateful to Florence Williams, Rick Ridgeway, and Pete McBride for trusting me with their own books, and to Nicole Moulton for her beautiful photography and Blair Anderson for her much-needed style help. Thank you to my Santa Fe family, particularly Kate Ferlic, who provided my own personal writing retreat in Taos. And deep love and thanks to my family back home in Nashville, beginning with Jane and Bill Coble, for instilling in us all such care for the natural world (except that blasted cormorant). I have learned how to love a piece of land from you.

Most of all, thank you to my husband, Win, who carried us on his back, as he always does, during the making of this book. And to our daughter, Camille, the animal lover, for whom the whole wide wilderness awaits. I love you both.

STAND UP FOR THE GILA

Keep the Gila Wild with your support of the following organizations:

GILA CONSERVATION COALITION / gilaconservation.org
GILA RESOURCES INFORMATION PROJECT / gilaresources.info/wp
UPPER GILA WATERSHED ALLIANCE / ugwa.org
AMERICAN RIVERS / americanrivers.org
NM WILD / nmwild.org
NEW MEXICO WILDLIFE FEDERATION / nmwildlife.org
THE CENTER FOR BIOLOGICAL DIVERSITY / biologicaldiversity.org
THE WILDERNESS SOCIETY / wilderness.org
WILDEARTH GUARDIANS / wildearthguardians.org

WILDEARTH GUARDIANS

WILDEARTH GUARDIANS PROTECTS AND RESTORES the wildlife, wild places, wild rivers, and health of the American West. We envision a world where wildlife and wild places are respected and valued and our world is sustainable for all beings. We believe in nature's inherent right to exist and thrive. We speak for the wild life, places, and waters that have been dominated and abused to serve the interests of a greedy few. Bit by bit, we are restoring the balance.

At the heart of our vision is a belief in the intrinsic rights of nature, the blessings of diversity, the critical role of bold action, and that citizens' voices are essential—on the streets, in the halls of Congress, and in the courtroom—to address the nature and climate crises. WildEarth Guardians nurtures an ethic of social and racial equity as central to the success of all of our work. Learn more about our mission and how you can help protect the West's wildest, diverse ecosystems at wildearthguardians.org.

TORREY HOUSE PRESS

VOICES FOR THE LAND

The economy is a wholly owned subsidiary of the environment, not the other way around.
—Senator Gaylord Nelson, founder of Earth Day

Torrey House Press publishes books at the intersection of the literary arts and environmental advocacy. THP authors explore the diversity of human experiences with the environment and engage community in conversations about landscape, literature, and the future of our ever-changing planet, inspiring action toward a more just world. We believe that lively, contemporary literature is at the cutting edge of social change. We seek to inform, expand, and reshape the dialogue on environmental justice and stewardship for the human and more-than-human world by elevating literary excellence from diverse voices.

Visit www.torreyhouse.org for reading group discussion guides, author interviews, and more.

As a 501(c)(3) nonprofit publisher, our work is made possible by generous donations from readers like you.

This book was made possible by a generous donation from Patagonia© and a partnership with WildEarth Guardians. Torrey House Press is supported by Back of Beyond Books, the King's English Bookshop, Maria's Bookshop, the Jeffrey S. & Helen H. Cardon Foundation, the Sam & Diane Stewart Family Foundation, the Barker Foundation, Diana Allison, Klaus Bielefeldt, Laurie Hilyer, Shelby Tisdale, Kirtly Parker Jones, Robert Aagard & Camille Bailey Aagard, Kif Augustine Adams & Stirling Adams, Rose Chilcoat & Mark Franklin, Jerome Cooney & Laura Storjohann, Linc Cornell & Lois Cornell, Susan Cushman & Charlie Quimby, Betsy Gaines Quammen & David Quammen, the Utah Division of Arts & Museums, Utah Humanities, the National Endowment for the Humanities, the National Endowment for the Arts, the Salt Lake City Arts Council, and Salt Lake County Zoo, Arts & Parks. Our thanks to individual donors, members, and the Torrey House Press board of directors for their valued support.

Join the Torrey House Press family and give today at www.torreyhouse.org/give.